This Is Why I D.A.N.C.E.

Discover. Accomplish. Nourish. Create. Embrace.

D1598621

Written by Amara Riccio

Co-Written and edited by
Jessica Giannone

NEWMAN SPRINGS PUBLISHING
320 Broad Street
Red Bank, NJ 07701

First originally published by Newman Springs Publishing 2020

ISBN 978-1-63692-104-4 (Paperback)
ISBN 978-1-63692-105-1 (Digital)

Printed in the United States of America

Dedication

THIS BOOK IS DEDICATED TO my late uncle Neil, my number 1 fan, who always believed in me. He was the one who encouraged me to write this book. He gave me the confidence to speak up for myself and assured me I was going to achieve my dream, no matter what.

***

My work is in honor of every being I met through my family's nonprofit organization, Riccio Pick-Me-Ups; all my friends mentioned in this book; all supporters, caregivers; and every person reading this today.

To those lost in unexpected tragedies such as the COVID-19 crisis, 9/11, accidents, mental health-related deaths, and all those fighting each day to live.

In most loving memory of Grandma Mary Giannone, Papa Biagio Giannone, Granny Mary Zampardi, Mary and Michael Riccio Jr. and Sr., Aunt Dorothy Filosa, grandparents Lawrence and Marie Riccio, godfather Tommy Amodeo, neighbor Sue Meeker, and former Howell mayor Bob Walsh.

To all the young angels gone way too soon, including my cousin Michael Salvo; Kean University's Amelia Gaillard; Howell High School's Parker Drake; special angels I met: Thomas Wakeham, Karisa Pitre, Jesse Garret Green, and Amy Bac; and local child angels Jake Hoing and Mya Lin Terry.

Uncle Neil (left) and Uncle Jimmy (right) at
Amara's high school graduation party, 2013

Acknowledgments

A COLOSSAL HUG IN GRATITUDE goes out to my extraordinary parents, Lori and Larry, for doing their best to give me the greatest life possible, allowing me to use all the abilities I have. They deserve most of the credit for the person I am today, especially my mom. I don't thank you enough. I greatly appreciate how you raised my genuine, kind, energetic, and passionate brothers.

A huge thank you to my cousin Jessica "Soul Sister" Giannone for turning this dream into a reality. She is my ultimate inspiration for all my creative pursuits; I am blessed to have her constant support throughout this journey. Thank you to Jessica's parents (my Aunt Kathy and Uncle Anthony) for their unconditional love and support. To my crazy, unique, and loving uncles Frankie and Jamie for always sending their positive vibes my way. To my dad's sister, Aunt Lauren, thank you for being a role model of loyalty.

A shout-out to Uncle Jimmy Genovese, who inspires me to find humor and positivity in everything; to Aunt Lucy, who shows me age is just a number; and to all of my Riccio and Giannone cousins for supporting my mission to help others throughout the years.

With gratitude to the following:

- Brain Injury Alliance of New Jersey, North Brunswick Township, New Jersey
- Children's Specialized Hospital, New Brunswick and Toms River, New Jersey

- K. Hovnanian Children's Hospital (Jersey Shore University Medical Center), Neptune City, New Jersey
- Hospital at SUNY Downstate Medical Center, Brooklyn, New York
- Ocean's Harbor House (youth shelter), Toms River, New Jersey
- Shore Rehabilitation Institute, Brick Township, New Jersey
- Preferred Home Health Care & Nursing Services (Nurse Athalie), Eatontown, New Jersey
- Hackensack Meridian Health, Hackensack, New Jersey
- Good Shepherd Rehabilitation, Allentown, Pennsylvania
- Rising Treetops at Oakhurst (camp), Oakhurst, New Jersey
- The Dream Factory of the Jersey Shore, Wall, New Jersey
- PeaceLove CREATORS Program, Pawtucket, Rhode Island
- Yoga Peace Kula, Howell, New Jersey
- Tull Family Foundation, Pittsburgh, Pennsylvania
- Howell Township Police Department, Howell, New Jersey
- St. Veronica Church, Howell, New Jersey

Education

- Howell High School (special thanks to my English teacher Mary Ennis Collins and case worker Julie Adkins), Howell, New Jersey
- School of Health and Human Performance, Recreation Administration, and Therapeutic Recreation departments (adviser Dr. Fran Daly and all professors), Kean University, Union, New Jersey
- Expressive Therapies Studies (graduate) (adviser Dr. Angelica Pinna-Perez), Lesley University, Cambridge, Massachusetts

Lastly, thanks to my sixth grade English teacher Karen Manney, Howell High School nurse Eileen Eccleston, acting professor Ernest Wiggens, dance teacher Dawn Toledo-Clayton, my young dance student Brandon Gonzalez, pediatrician Dr. Visconti, nurse Katie

Shanley, photographer Jabriel Roberts (Pitched by Pat Photography), and all fellow classmates, therapists, writers, dancers, musicians, artists, educators, and health care workers who helped inspire this book.

I'm inspired by everyone I've connected with through Riccio Pick-Me-Ups, including Ryan Magnotta, Bobby Marshall, Jessica Jester, Amy Raezer, Ronald Brooks, Maria Johnson, Nicolette Palazzo, and the Cosgrove, Zampardi, Bernstein, Paris, Senanakye, Abbazia, Stillwell, Teat, and Zuppardo families, just to name a few…

Muchas gracias; *grazie*; thank you from the bottom of my heart. You are part of the reason why I dance.

Editor's Note

"Just as bad things can happen so quickly, good things can happen so quickly…"
—Amara Elise Riccio

IN THIS PUZZLING LIFE, IT's often difficult to process a simple yet compelling insight such as this. When things go wrong, most of us don't anticipate a positive turnaround. We might question why events occur, wonder when (or if) our circumstances will get better, and worry we will have to accept a situation that will seemingly weigh us down for the foreseeable future.

I do believe, of course, that we must process the bad; allow it to be acknowledged and passed. The idea of life taking a spin into questionable territory in an instant…it's scary and inevitable. However, there's comfort in knowing something beautiful is just as easily attainable—and likely; always around the corner. Instead of anticipating the worst, there's grace in searching for the best. There is always the mystical, grand chance that a gift—a strength; an understanding—will pay a visit to us, if only we open our eyes.

Amara embeds this reminder of hope into my life every single day. When she was initially comatose from her accident, I didn't truly believe she would never return to us. I don't think this mindset was necessarily denial. I think we all simply knew; we felt it, even though the odds were not good. It was unlikely she would recover, never mind lead a semi-normal life. Yet life surprises us.

Her recovery was one thing, by definition: a miracle. As I watched her progress amazingly into her teens, and eventually adulthood, I couldn't shake the feeling that she was supposed to (from an existential standpoint) do something; something beyond herself. She, of course, spent many years changing lives through her charity—but also merely by being herself. She has so much more to give yet.

Her insights and experiences from her recent regression have changed her in profound ways. A spark has been ignited. I hope it can "enlighten" you too.

***

This book has been a journey in itself. Amara, despite her physical limitations with typing and communicating, has managed to carry a message across the confines of space into our hearts. I don't know if I could ever have it in me to accomplish what she has with this work of grit, under the same circumstances. As an able-bodied, fortunate young woman, it has been a struggle for me to edit and publish this book entirely alone. I know I could have asked for help, but some voice inside me said, "If Amara can push through individual battles every day, how amazing would it be for the two of us to tackle this feat solely together?" It's our tiny but magnificent demonstration of spirit.

We collaborated on this almost entirely without speaking. Through all the mixed batches of e-mails, persistent Google Docs comments, sporadic Facebook messages, and haphazard text messages, we somehow brought a vision to life. All the crazy hours, periods of doubt, and endless months of focus have morphed into a tangible expression of faith.

Contrary to what would be expected, Amara's writing was actually easier for me to get through than that of most people because her ideas resonate with me in such a natural way. Despite some unexpected setbacks, which complicated our firm deadline of June 1 (the anniversary of Amara's accident), Amara has pushed me forward. She has lifted me up, giving me a sense of purpose. Focusing on someone else wholeheartedly has taught me that we truly do "rise by lifting others."[1]

This book has transformed into something that means so much more than it would have, precisely because of unforeseen misfortunes. Our Uncle Neil's passing, for example, borrowed our time, but he changed the course of this book. The last-minute uncertainties with proofreaders forced me to rethink Amara's words once again. These tokens of change made me realize how fluid we must be; in our mentality, and in life. Things don't always go according to plan, and that's a blessing.

The mind of Amara shines through in these pages, and it's contagious like a smile. She inspired me to keep writing. You may notice a lot of old quotes of mine throughout the book (which Amara INSISTED I include), as well as other noted input from myself. We should clarify that although Amara and I prefer to distinguish our own thoughts and ideas, even when we share creations, we didn't indicate every instance of this. I have expanded on some of Amara's messages, as well as edited some previously published posts for clarity. However, what you're reading is direct from Amara's heart; no filter. Throughout this book, we worked together to weave these words into one humble albeit powerful voice. I must say Amara's wisdom has genuinely riveted me to my core. It amazes me every day how much her mind and words throughout this journey have influenced me on my own.

Now, I continue to watch Amara grow. Her writing, humor, and wits seem to get better each day. Some may say her brain is compensating for her other limitations, but I believe she was naturally meant to flourish in these years because she is learning so much; utilizing all her knowledge in a way that matters more than it ever has. Her soul is nourished with an extra kiss of love.

In concluding words, this book has personally allowed me to do the following:

Discover: what I'm capable of, in addition to illuminating insights from Amara, which tickle me with knowledge.
Accomplish: a feat I never thought was possible on my own.
Nourish: my soul with what I love the most.

Create: the most important thing I ever dreamed of.

Embrace: the process of the good, the bad, and the unknown; the dance...

Contents

This Is Why

Did you ever feel as if hope was defeating the impossible?
When someone or something knocks you way down a
hill, you have to jump higher than the hill itself.

THIS WAS A QUOTE FROM my twelve-year-old self a month before I found out what hope really is. All my life, I had a passion to spread happiness to people by sharing my love for writing, dance, and the creative arts. The driving force of this book is my life experience, but you'll find it's a different type of autobiography. I am who I am because of a multitude of individuals and life forces. These people, along with extraordinary circumstances, have shaped my heart. Now I'm pouring it out onto these pages.

It's incredible how things come to pass.

***

When all your dreams seemed crushed, in reality it's
the beginning of your aspirations...maybe one day I
will have published books.

It has been more than a decade since I wrote that statement for an essay in seventh grade, and my dream has become a reality, despite falling down that metaphorical hill.

I have climbed up dancing.

This allowed me to spread hope to others because I realized the power of "Why me?" is truly "Why not?" Before we begin, is there something in your life that made you say "Why me?" Dwell on how you can turn that doubt into "Why not?"

Amara flipping at the Star Systems dance competition, 2008

ℐ...

On June 22, 1995, I was born in Staten Island, New York (the daughter of two amazing Italian American parents). I have two brothers: Robert, who is sixteen months younger than me, and Lawrence, who is twenty months older. I was brought up by an extremely supportive family, filled with love and opportunity, allowing me the chance to live life to the fullest. They supported me in all my endeavors—the major ones being dance and acrobatic gymnastics.

Three weeks before my thirteenth birthday, I was struck by a car on the way to my second dance recital of the day. I sustained severe traumatic brain injury (TBI),[2] specifically a left frontal lobe fracture and diffuse axonal shearing[3] (cellular injury that affects the whole brain). I was in a coma for nine days, spent months in hospitals, had a setback, and underwent several years of therapy. Most importantly, however, I learned how precious life is. My ability to dance was not lost—just altered.

I have made many strides throughout the years. Most notably, I started my own charity. In 2011, with the encouragement from my generous mother, I created Riccio Pick-Me-Ups, a nonprofit organization to help give recreational, emotional, financial, and educational support to families facing medical hardships.

During my freshman year of college on New Year's Eve of 2013, I had an epiphany; a theory; a motto of a word that seemed to define me for most of my life. This acronym is almost like a personal guide (we can call it guiDANCE), which can be utilized and adapted to everyone's lives. This creation has been shared with hundreds of people throughout the New Jersey and New York area, as well as nationwide, through presentations, writings, talks, and raps, and in casual, everyday situations:

> I believe that everyone has—or will have—a chance to D.A.N.C.E. **Discover** abilities, **Accomplish** goals, **Nourish** the soul, **Create** something totally new, and **Embrace** life fully through.

This motto was put to my own test in the fall of 2017 when I had what I thought was prolonged laryngitis with increased brain injury symptoms due to stress. I graduated college with a BA in therapeutic recreation and became a certified therapeutic recreation specialist (CTRS). I was working three part-times jobs and enrolled in graduate school for expressive arts therapy/counseling. I had to live up to my testimony, as I had two and a half years of doctor visits, eight hospital/rehabilitation stays, and countless therapy for having a rare, unknown, and severe neurological disorder. Symptoms are classified as diffuse encephalopathic slowing[4] and progressive ataxia,[5] along with pseudobulbar syndrome,[6] and upper motor cranial nerve[7] damage of the face, neck, throat, and tongue. This greatly impacts muscle control and balance in my entire body, taking away my ability to walk, talk, swallow, see with both eyes together, sit, smile, and even control bladder/bowel.

I need 24-7 care. Thanks to my mom, I can be home (along with nurses eight hours a day, when they show). My mom wakes up several times a night to reposition me and perform Kangaroo feeding pump[8] changes. The stimulation makes me scream involuntarily, and it pains me to cause so much stress. Still, she tries her best to be calm, and she helps me push on.

To my mom and all the caregivers out there: know your loved ones appreciate you more than they communicate. I know without my mom, I would probably be in a nursing home, where I would eventually die. (During one instance at a nursing home, a week of respite from my parents actually turned into a fight to live. It wasn't the staff's fault. It's just the system.) I am grateful always.

In February of 2020, chronic microbleeding was shown for the first time around my brain. Toxic iron buildup[9] may be part of the cause. Regardless, nothing will steal my love away.

Though my life story can be intense to take in (even for me), this book is intended to be a feel-good read: a medley of some of my thoughts, feelings, education, expressive poems, blog posts from my journey, and short personal stories. I'm also featuring those who inspire me—all with some humor to help you D.A.N.C.E. There will be many connections to colors, nature, words, psychology, health, art, and recreation throughout the book, along with the use of various literary devices (and puns galore!).

You are never too old or too young to make a difference. Struggles and mistakes do not define us, though they do help create us. These scars can be stars if we create our own definitions, sharing our bright sparkle within.

This is how and why I D.A.N.C.E.

Amara and mom, 2018

Part 1
Discover

*Discover: to make known or visible; to obtain sight
or knowledge of for the first time; to find out.*[10]

AT FOUR YEARS OLD, I jumped high to be able to see myself in the mirror.

"Hello, world, this is me! What should I be?"

"Everything is so big, and I am so small. How do I make sense of it all?"

A decade later, at age fourteen, my reflection was shown a miracle.

"Wow. I almost left."

"There's so much to learn, so much to do. I have another chance to get to know me—and you too!"

"OK, OK, I'm ready... Here I go. Let's start the show!"

Jumping another decade, at age twenty-four, my mirror of ideas was called to come to life again.

Have you ever wondered how and why you were put here on this earth? The evolution of humanity is a mystery in itself. With that inevitable question put aside, most of us know how living creatures produce, allowing generations to expand. The point is, we are all born babies. No one skips a step. Every plant starts as a seed planted in the dirt. The first few years of life are where most of our discovery occurs.

Some people say a child's brain is like a sponge. Well, some sponges are more worn out than others, depending on overall health and environmental circumstances. However, we all have the greatest capacity to absorb information when we are young. As children grow, their brains are still sponges, but they're filled up with information—some unfortunately traumatizing and others very healthy.

Discovery of emotions and behaviors is often a process that can be difficult for us to understand in youth. Teenage years are often the most confusing (that's an understatement) and the time where many individuals truly find out who they are or who they want to be. One does not enter the discovery alone, but with the support and guidance of many individuals. This includes parents, family members, friends, teachers, coaches, doctors, and whoever else is around a child. By the time young adulthood comes around, many believe they have it all figured out.

Since grade school, I always thought to myself, "There's so much I know…how much more is there, really?" Well, tomorrow, I will be telling my young self, "Oh, honey…you have no idea." I was writing this book in the middle of discovering life, but I am grateful that my education, conversations with others, and life experiences have given me the tools to explain my philosophy of dance. The following chapters will explain different aspects of the discovery process with examples from my life, along with ways you can begin your D.A.N.C.E.

Lawrence, Jessica, Amara, Robbie, and cousin Jack
performing for family during the holidays, 2000

Unbelievable! This is so unbelievable. I can't believe it…but it's real. (Uncle Neil Giannone)

Chapter 1
People, Places, and Things

Discovery of something's true essence is essential in order to interpret, analyze, theorize, and move forward in D.A.N.C.E. That is why it's the first step.

Robert holding Hani Jay, Amara holding Baboo,
Lawrence holding Calla Jo, Christmas 2016

IMAGINE THAT YOU ARE A minuscule ant walking through a ginormous city filled with sky-high buildings and billions of other ginormous animals. In comparison to the size of the world and the amount of people, places, and things in it, each one of us can wind up like that ant. We can be squished and forgotten by society. Yet we are *Homo sapiens*—the most advanced in the animal kingdom on earth, our home. With this in mind, instead of being an ant, we can share our own anthems with the world.

Our anthems are written and sung by the places, people, and things that influence our world. My anthem was first tuned by my mother, whose heart beats because of her mother, and so on. There are many instruments that harmonize or—at least attempt to—create our individual songs. The diversity of our country and universe is what keeps it spinning 'round. Family members share the closest stories to us; even then, it's totally unique.

Families are the first forms of people most of us encounter and spend time with more than anyone else. Mothers often create, sustain, and guide their babies to live their best lives. My mamma, grandma, and generations before have kept the family dancing every day. My mother is a special education teacher, and my dad is an oncology pharmacist. Their passion for their professions and humanity has helped me discover my purpose too.

Just like every living thing, families grow and change, yet some things still stay the same. I discovered morals and values from my family, which I always live by. Some of these values include giving, education, recreation, "family comes first," loyalty in friendship, and eternal faith. I make discoveries through a variety of experiences with my parents, brothers, uncles, aunts, and cousins.

I was brought up in an educated, middle-class environment, though many times living paycheck to paycheck (like most of America). However, I had all the things I needed and MUCH more. The most important thing I had was LOVE. Like many families and individuals, we experienced hardships and made it through the hospitals, the crazy car rides, the tears, the storms—all of it together. Each individual family member's fight is always the entire family's fight.

With this fighting spirit, the desire to make an impact is contagious throughout our family. My mom has dedicated her life to being a strong advocate for the needs of my brothers and I, along with others in the disability community. The rest of the family has followed suit. Navigating the health care/education world is not easy, but it's possible with strong forces like my parents. When people say I am amazing, my response is: it's because of the "maze" of my life that my family has gone through together; the maze of celebrations, grievances, tragedies, failures, and successes. I owe everything to them, starting with my ancestors in heaven.

Creativity, compassion, humor, and intellect are in my genetic makeup, despite mutations that may come with it. If I tell my mom that her shirt is inside out or her pants are backward, she will remind us that she was born backward in a doctor's office. She says "It's good luck," so she will not change it. (My mom is a difficult woman, in a positive way, because she is feisty and will not take no for an answer when it comes to something she is passionate about). Everyone in my family is very stubborn, including me, so that does cause heated conflicts, which we always forgive and move on from.

My grandma was also stubborn, funny, and compassionate. My mom lives through her words and actions. I see that in my great-uncle Jimmy as well, the most joyful person I know. Even before my illness, he would say, "What's the 'mada' with Amara?" or sing "The sun will come out... Amara" in the tune of "Tomorrow" from *Annie*. He is the only living sibling on my grandma's side, living with the strongest spirit and love.

My cousin Jessica and I are more like soul sisters. We have been creating and philosophizing together since day 1. The bond we share isn't just a result of having similar values, passions, and thought processes (as silly as that sounds). It's deeper than that. We seem to know the other's feelings (most of the time) and share a sisterly energy that transcends our physical barriers. We are both protective of each other (even when other family members get in criticism mode), and we'll always have each other's backs. The love we share of performing, writing, helping others, puns/wordplay, games, music, goofiness, and creativity is a gift we will cherish for all our days, young or old.

We all have common bonds and differences that set us apart. Although many of my family members look alike and have similar ideas, we are all so distinct from one another. My uncles (my mom's four brothers) are all comically different. Their quirky characters cause some (entertaining) chaos in the family. I love each of them dearly, even if I strongly dislike their differing views and actions sometimes, just like with anyone else.

Robert and I, for instance, have done almost everything together: same school, same work, same home. We have different friends and interests, yet we're both driven, comedic, and loving. As far as obvious differences go, Rob is a procrastinator, and I have to get work done right away! He is an extreme extrovert, and I enjoy my alone time for creativity. Rob is so much like my mom and her brothers; I am more quirky like my father. Regardless of similarities and differences, I learn many lessons from my family, as well as from friends and other people around me.

With all this in mind, I learned that love can be the root of hate and choice can be the cause of fate. To display anger toward another person is often simply the result of concern and frustration that the anger-ridden person has. Unfortunately, violence can be a common consequence of this affection. Someone who has not experienced what true love is can, many times, experience deeds of hate. This is why spreading love to all individuals is so important. This idea can be taken in the context of the extreme or even in typical circumstances like family arguments and sibling rivalries.

Lawrence has autism[11] and bipolar disorder.[12] He was my first best friend and my parents' firstborn child—strong, intelligent, and beautiful. He has an unbelievably larger-than-life personality and love for his family. However, when he is in his psychosis state, he rages on the things and people he loves most, including himself. To many, this would look like hate (he will even say "I hate you"). These actions and words are really just a display of love to test its conditions. Let me tell you—his love is unconditional, just as ours is for him. To this day, Lawrence still accepts me, even though I have a different voice. (Initially, he would ask, "What's wrong with Amara?" and "When is her voice coming back?"). It took him two years, but he somehow understands now. Normally, this drastic change would throw him off, but our bond is stronger than physical limits and illusions. My dad has also grown a special bond with Lawrence through the years, and their relationship is truly admirable.

Despite my family and extended family experiencing conflicts and uncontrollable hardships, we have somehow become boats that stay afloat with an anchor of love. This love passes on through generations. Family is not only defined by the genes in our blood but by the individuals in our lives who love even through the stickiest of mud.

As we grow up, we discover the people outside our families, some who share love like family. The value of a relationship is what makes it like that of a family, not just the DNA. Many friends come and go, but there are some who stay in our lives for the rest of our days.

Most of my childhood friends and I went our separate ways in our teenage years, but I do have a special few who have stuck around. I want to acknowledge my great friend, Jillian, who has supported me since sixth grade. Our bond is built on education and helping others.

Jillian and my longest close friend, Ashley, were the ones who helped my organization expand by being our first volunteers. They are truly extraordinary young women. Jillian shows me true friends do not have to be classic "do everything together" besties to have a lasting friendship. Our bond has lasted longer than those I've had with others who I thought were my "best friends." I know she will always be in my life.

Love the People

A common phrase you may hear from others—or in your mind—is "I hate people." This thought process occurs when the majority of people are generalized based off a few individuals in a person's life who did, or continue to do, things that bring about hostile emotions. As much as I would like to, I cannot take these emotions and feelings toward others away from you. Think of people like diamonds. No matter how irritating others can be, they are diamonds in the rough. Shine like that diamond and you will find other gems too. These gems can become friends.

Finding genuine friendships is not easy. I learned throughout the years that the greatest friendships happen unexpectedly. Sometimes people grow on you. You may not connect in the beginning, and then you suddenly (or gradually) become closer. Several of the people whom I connected with in my life instantly became my greatest friends. These friendships sail across many waters. Some drift away, and others stay on the same boat, supporting us for life.

Pop-Ups

Have you ever had friends of your family whom you basically considered family? During my youth, at the hospital where my dad worked, he met people who would later become, as my uncle says, the greatest pop-ups. I grew up with the lovable Levy family: Neal, Vivian, and baby Michelle, who has now graduated from college! Together, we celebrated, struggled, grieved, laughed, and got through all the things that popped in life, even the corny, non-buttery moments. Vivian became my godmother for my confirmation because she has been the most consistent "family" member. Michelle became the little sister I always wanted. She is a Type 1 diabetes[13] warrior who never gives up on anything, and she found her passion for baking in high school. Needless to say, my godfamily reminds me how sweet life can be. I love these people—no sugarcoating needed.

Through Summers and Ashes

It was October of 2004 when I was in fourth grade. I moved to New Jersey and started a new school. The first person I started talking to became my best friend. We loved playing with dolls, singing, playing with kitties, and putting on elaborate home productions. Ironically, the day before my accident, I was dancing all day to celebrate her bat mitzvah. Through the ashes, and even summertime, I know I always have my girl, Ashley. In fifth grade (the year of girl drama), I met a sweet, shy little girl named Summer, and no one could break our bond, even though they tried. We loved doing art and being super silly together. She warmed my heart through all the seasons and summers.

These girls, and one unique, supportive friend from middle school, are the only ones who stuck around after my accident. Things started heating up through the high school and college years in their personal lives, burning parts of our friendships as we disconnected. I realized that true friends always do come back together at some point. I wish all my childhood friends the best, and I am thankful for

Ashley, Jillian, and all those who still pop in and out once in a while, almost like nothing's changed.

***

Animals can be the best companions as well. I am a huge believer in therapy and service animals. My cats make the purr-fect addition to my family. My sister-angel Holly, sweet one-eyed wonder Hani Jay, three-legged warrior Baboo, curious booty girl Calla Jo, and playful Sunny Bo complete a piece of my heart that is irreplaceable.

> Family can be a human, animal, or any special thing
> Those special friends that make our soul sing
> Family is completely original
> Whether or not traditional

We know that the power of people sharing, caring, and spending time together is priceless. People create the feeling, the atmosphere, and the vibe of places and things. You can be in a horrible place but have the best moments, or vice versa. Oftentimes, I've had more enjoyable moments in my hospital room with friends and family than on some vacations.

Natural Abilities (June 3, 2018)

Throughout my four-and-a-half-month hospital stay in 2017 and 2018, I was able to stay lovABLE, danceABLE, and adoreABLE because of the support of my parents, loved ones, those who worked with me, and even strangers. Dances are more enjoyable with others. My therapists, teachers, and other health care professionals have been a huge part of my life, and I'm forever grateful. Nevertheless, I cannot express enough the importance of environmental factors that contribute to one's well-being. Although it does not describe everything.

Sunny days tend to make people feel happier, but that's not the only contributor to one's well-being. I live by this famous Vivian

Greene quote: "Life isn't about waiting for the storm to pass... It's about learning to dance in the rain."

Time on earth is too short to wait around for the storms to stop, so I learned to just find a different way to dance. Nature has always inspired me because I feel connected through it all. It explains things that words cannot simply through the processes and cycles of life. The seasons and animals show us change is beautiful—just look at butterflies. The weather embodies beauty after disaster, like a rainbow after a torrential storm.

By definition, *nature* is[14]

- the inherent character or basic constitution of a person or thing; essence;
- a creative and controlling force in the universe;
- an inner force (such as instinct, appetite, desire) or the sum of such forces in an individual;
- the external world in its entirety;
- humankind's original or natural condition;
- the genetically controlled qualities of an organism; and
- natural scenery.

Both the nature in me and nurture from my support system have allowed me to work diligently during my decade after sustaining a severe TBI so I could enjoy my life dancing in the gardens, forests, cities, and woods, embracing life as a human fairy. Due to all this, after a plethora of medical tests, it was discovered that I was bitten by a rare infected mosquito, which was infected by a deceased bird (West Nile virus), giving me an extremely rare, untreatable, and debilitating illness. This was apparently the cause of my latest setback. I guess it goes to show how a human spirit can fly like a fairy, even when life is not fair.

> As we unwind from the day, we often recount the high points, the low points, and a dose of the occurrences in between. We have 24 hours' worth

of moments to weed through, yet a lifetime of memories still follows us for days to come. Whichever moments sprout up in our minds, they're the results of all the seeds we've planted in the past, mushed into one weathered bunch, and constantly changing with the seasons. Sometimes you have to get your hands dirty and be thrust into the rocky ground to create something truly beautiful. We're always looking toward the sun. (Jessica Giannone)

How have your family and friends affected the discovery of yourself, your life, and your external environment?

Chapter 2
Diversity

Differences in all living things defy the rules in math; they are actually positive additions that create the equation for life, making it greater.

WE ALL FIT INTO LIFE'S equation. If our properties were all the same, not only would it be extremely boring, but there would be so many empty roles and not enough good actors/actresses to fill them. That's why we are all created wonderfully unique. Each animal, plant, and human creature needs diversity for a sustainable life.

Without getting too scientific, just think about it. Each flower and animal, even of the same breed, is different in some way, and no two snowflakes are alike. There is even diversity in each individual culture. Race and ethnicity are permanent. Economic status, religion, abilities, sexual preference, and even gender can change. My personal diversity comes from my various stages of physical abilities and experiences.

I mentioned in an earlier chapter how differences in individuals start to become noticed within families. My brother Lawrence acted very differently from my younger brother and me. It does not mean something is wrong with him. He does many things right. Despite Lawrence's autism, I learned to appreciate his abilities and personality and to love him for everything he is. With the help of my mom, I learned to accept the abilities of others.

Attending college at Kean University, in addition to a summer graduate program at Lesley University, has helped me experience diversity—specifically the power, privilege, and oppression that comes along with it. There is pain, suffering, and injustice in this world. The truth is, we are not all born with equal opportunities. Due to societal influence, even though I try to feel the beat with everyone, I realized stereotypes often beat us down, even beneath our consciousness.

I used to have a real hippie mindset of everything—peace, love, one race, and one love—which I became less attached to, becoming a "leggie" after some education. It became evident to me that the world isn't always so simple. Each individual is ingrained with genetics, including cultural experiences, that are passed down generationally. Something that causes discrimination in a society that one cannot change makes one oppressed. So if someone does not experience this discrimination, he or she is privileged.

I am privileged from my race, my family, and the opportunities given to me along the way. Based on my experience making connections with people from all walks of life, I think the best way to immerse yourself in diversity is to talk and, more importantly, listen to others of a wide array of ages, cultural backgrounds, religions, political views, genders, etc. Minorities seem to be becoming more of a majority because it seems like most people have at least one thing that classifies them as a minority. Realistically, any kind of group can be oppressed in society, including women. There's always a group someone will not fit into. I always felt strange being a misfit, but now I have no choice but to accept it due to my disability. We cannot dismiss the disabilities that exist, and we must distinguish these limitations from people as individuals.

According to the University of New Hampshire's Institute on Disability, "If people with disabilities were a formally recognized minority group, at 19 [percent] of the population, they would be the largest minority group in the United States."[15] Disabilities do not discriminate across cultures, yet even in the US, with the American Disabilities Act, people experience physical and attitudinal barriers everywhere. For example, even doctors' offices aren't physically accessible. I am limited in places to attend because of my new physical state, including dance studios. Public recreation facilities have kicked out my brother for being "disruptive" as a result of his autism. Many times, when my family goes to a restaurant, we are viewed as a group from the circus, which most people are not prepared to witness.

Most people are kind, but because everyone is fighting his or her own battle, that fight can punch you in the face (literally). My brother was punched in his face and pushed by a boyfriend of a girl because he said, "Hi, what's your name?" These moments do not happen on the regular, but as seen in the media, it's real. No one stepped in to help. Be the upstander, as you can help save a life and/ or make a difference to that person. We all deserve to feel worthy and loved.

Through all these experiences, volunteering in various places, working as a therapist, giving presentations in schools, being a patient in a hospital, and attending cultural events at schools, my exposure to the community branched the roots to my accepting attitude. In my school presentations, although I focus on disabilities, I start with a diversity exercise, which I have done in different schools and community workshops. It can be adapted by different populations. It is a nice visual to see how people do have core qualities in common: the desire to be loved, be happy, and to dream, despite any other differences.

Outside of personal connections, reading articles online from sites such as *The Mighty* help shine a light on illness, disability, and diversity. Most of our differences are unseen when we share a smile and compassion. We are all mysteries—with no need to be solved, especially not by the public.

We all have many pages in our own books, along with generational chapters. I always feel the need to explain myself because I want to advocate, educate, and be understood. I learned that I do not need to explain myself, nor does anyone need an explanation to be respected. Some individuals' stories are more closed than others. Their stories should still be honored. We truly never know what someone has been through, is going through, or where they will go.

"You crazy, disabled freak"
"You sick, queer, geek"

You hear words like that from society
From in your head; your anxiety
You are defined by more than one name
No reason for this shame

Disable the label…diselba lebla…
Disable the label…diselba lebla…

We each have a biopsychosocial[16] entity
Only you can create your identity
They say I'm out there
Let me tell you I'm here
You can stop and stare
I'm not gonna disappear

Disable the label…

Intention vs. impact
How do we comprehend
Opinion vs. fact
Until you're on the other end
This is not pretend…

We live in a world with stereotypes and prejudices
Hundreds of "isms" lie beneath our consciousness
This is not as good as it gets
Let's "yes"
Yes, let's

Disable the label with
Peace…love…peace and love…

I wrote these rap lyrics as part of a song about disabling stereotypical labels in July of 2017. I rapped while my friend sang. I forgot about it then remastered it with a new friend in graduate school, where I performed it at an arts café event.

Disabling the label is just about treating all people with the dignity they deserve. Each word has a connotation that can be degrading. I like to say it is more about positive character building than antibullying. My mom has also taught me "it's not exactly what you say, but how you say it." The first step to achieve this is helping people discover diversity and teaching people ways to respect one another. Also, those words listed above in the song do describe me, but it's about redefining them to reduce negative stigmas and letting other primary, more important characteristics shine greater.

> So much more than black and white
> Like a spectrum of light
> Now the world is seeing more of a rainbow
> Where do we go?

The diversity in people, places, and things around us encompasses the true beauty of the world we live in. Discover things around you. Listen to worldly events. Seeing people in need with my own eyes, through my own experiences, has helped me cultivate the following poem:

Social Justice (October 2015)

> I keep asking myself "Why?"
> The answer I receive is "It's just how life is"
> So it just is…just me…just us…?
>
> Walking down the street
> Wind in my hair, ground to my feet
>
> Feeling like I'm in a store, but I'm not
> Really, this is what we got?

This Is Why I D.A.N.C.E.

Like consumer packages in this society, everyone has a label
The meaning that's behind the words is what is not stable

Homeless, mental, alien, disabled, gay
Excuse me? HEY!

Not everyone fits in one box; it needs more space
Each so individually different in this amazing human race

What's the price?
The fight, of course, something's got to suffice

Like objects, sometimes it seems as if some creatures are
worth more
But we are all here to give, feel, live, laugh, love, and adore

Every element on this earth is made with purpose
So then why are people and things treated to feel worthless?

It's more than just words; it's actions that make the change
Let's put together the pieces of the world that seem so
strange

Protect the beauty of nature, our world, our land
Our animals, our creatures…we take a stand

For our people; populations who feel alone
We need open hearts, an open zone

We are the rainbow, not individual colors; no need for
separation
When the colors come together, we can bring in the
sun—integration

To help give health and wellness of each body, mind, and
soul

Because unfairness and inequality take a toll

So just I, I just…
I just believe together we will create a song
We all play along

With our own unique melodies
And I believe that one day we can all play in harmony
In unity:
Come on, this is an opportunity!

We have a powerful, beautiful voice
And a choice

It isn't "just is" or "just me" or "just you" or "just us," but
      just one liberty: justice for all
Justice for all.
That is the American call

The collective moments we discover—these unique forces—are when we begin to D.A.N.C.E. to our own beats.

***

In 2020, the world started reacting to injustice as incomprehensible racial brutalities were impacting communities. It breaks my heart to hear about injustices every day, yet my heart says we're coming together because the world has been uniting in acts of peace and love to fight the corrupt system, especially with LGBT pride and the Black Lives Matter movement. I think if we continue toward inclusive "dance" in our divine diversity, a change will come.

From Another Planet

I was hooked to IV fluids, freezing on Christmas Eve in a hospital bed, thankful for my breaths but confused about what was happening. My FROM (friend who could be my mom) was yelling at me because she was upset. Important realization: I know love comes in different forms; tough love being one of them. Okay, so I'll take it back to when our stars aligned at Kean University.

In my therapeutic recreation class, there was one other person who asked more questions and told more stories than I did. Our diverse backgrounds increased our interests in various subjects, leading us to speak up on topics regarding disability, aging, cultural competence, and therapeutic services. I realized this other person, Venus, comes from another planet, yet she is the most down-to-earth woman I know. She is a strong, independent African American woman, veteran, and (at that time) community recreation/health major. She is eighteen years older than me and has two daughters. One is a teenager, Destinee, whom I became friends with after she walked me back to my dorm one icy evening.

I guess because I'm close with my mom, I sometimes befriend people who fill that role, especially when she is not around. Venus always made sure I was safe. Our families became amazing friends. Despite differences, we are more alike, and that's what we believe globally unites us. The space between the stars, planets, and us is smaller than you might think. I do not know what Mars is like, but Venus is pretty out-of-this-world awesome!

***

As Jessica adds:

Diversity doesn't just deal with disabilities and culture. It comes from within. It is important to emphasize the "mystery" some of us creatives create; how many people rule out imaginative thinking as irrational or "too much;" how this should not be the case; why the world needs minds like ours...

> *"I appreciate art, music, and dance. I really do, and you know it. People like you, Jessica, and those friends of yours... I respect what you do. But it's*

like you're traveling to another planet in your mind
(*makes weird noises*), and I just don't understand
all that "creativity" stuff. Not for me." (Uncle Neil
Giannone)

The people who don't understand creativity may just be afraid—of
their own minds. Travelling to these depths takes courage. I think a lot of
people think it's unnecessary. But for people like us, it's crucial. I try not
to judge and make assumptions about people who aren't creative, even
though a lot of the time, they judge us. But Uncle Neil always praised
and admired us for it. I don't blame anyone for turning their cheek to
expressive arts. They just don't understand, is all.
There is so much to explore.

(We will revisit creativity in Part 4: Create. We all have **different** outlets and creativity within us yearning to come out.)

*When did you first discover differences within yourself, your
family, your community, and beyond? Do you recognize your own
stereotypes? Is there more you want to learn about others who are
different from you?

Chapter 3
Passion

The meaning of life is to find your own special meaning. Find it, love it, never let go of it. We all have that passion and fire found inside our hearts, found deep inside where all of our love gives our lives pure purpose. Set a match & start those flames. For the true beauty is the passions & love inside your heart.

—Delanie Cosgrove

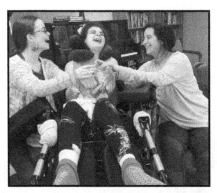

Amara's friends Delanie (left) and Sophia (right) making a clay heart at Good Shepherd Rehabilitation, April 2018

How DOES ONE FIND THAT burning desire in his or her heart? Well, developing a passion starts with an interest in a person, thing, or activity. This can start at a very young age or develop later in life.

This is the first *P* to my Four *P*s of Success: **Passion, Patience, Perseverance,** and **Play**.

I had a passion for the arts and giving to others ever since I can remember. I practiced my dancing and writing, never giving up. Even when I failed, I had fun doing it. I think passion leads to talent. Even if you are not the most skilled at a particular activity, if you love it, that's all that matters. Passionate people inspire passion in others. This is why many members of families have similar passions. My cousin Jessica had put together family shows with my brothers and I since we were around the age of three. In her words: "I believe in survival of the passionate."

When I was younger, peers would make fun of me for my passionate actions. When I read in class, I liked to act like the book characters, and I was always dancing, even without music. I learned that some people will talk because they really have nothing else better to do than make comparisons and put you down. This is just a tool to help you get back up to be even more passionate and determined! I know in my life, I have always been my own biggest critic due to comparisons.

> I learned to become inspired when thoughts in my head fired: Motivation
> "I want to do that"; no need for fighting. I'm not a cat
> OK, I just need to tell myself perfection is a perception
> It's all about being the best you can be; you do you, and I'll do me

Some passions are more obvious than others. Some are specific sports, activities, education, or actions that turn into professions. A person may have a passion for working with children, older adults, or animals, for example. This may not be considered talent, but it's a quality that influences the person in his or her future career. The passion might only be noticed in the moments the individual is in his or her element, but many times, this passion carries over to everything the person does. Anyone can be trained to do a job, play a game, or learn to sing, but the passion is what sets one person apart from another. It becomes a part of someone. It's something that makes him or her unique and feel special. Sharing this gift with others will expand this passion and be a gift to others as well.

Countless other examples: musicians can sing to people in hospitals, chefs can cook for soup kitchens, athletes can share their passions with youth, inventors can develop products to help solve problems, and artists can create art to lift spirits. One thing all successful individuals have is passion. It creates the drive to accelerate down the highway of life. Despite many bumps in the road, detours, and U-turns, I truly believe if you love something strong enough, it will drive you on the path your heart desires.

As previously mentioned, my love for the arts began when my cousin Jessica developed home productions at family gatherings. It increased when I witnessed and experienced its healing properties in hospitals from both angles—me as a patient and a professional. I realized it was more than just the outside sparkles and show; it sparkled the inner soul that radiated within. True passion always feels exciting. The activity is rarely bothersome, even during stressful situations. Even when I was exhausted or feeling sick and still running programs, I was able to keep going strong because I was so in love with my work.

There are few things a central nervous system disorder (or any condition) can take away from a person, and one of those things is, of course, passion. My mom said that even in a coma, I was dancing with the right side of my body in my dreams. During both of my rehabilitations, I wrote poems, made bracelets, constructed clay sculptures, sang songs, and danced. All this was done in an adaptive way, but I still did it! Passion is the stepping-stone to discovery of the self and accomplishments. It kept me going strong and helped others discover their passions too.

Passion, itself, is not innate. It's an elusive, fickle gift that we must perpetuate through the darkness. But our resources are here…in the form of whispering

embers. Memories of our feats; awareness of our pos-
sibilities and strengths; comfort in the inevitability
of change. The courage to do so. Liberation. (Jessica
Giannone)

Beauty and the Beast

In July of 2012, I met a beautiful soul sister (number 1 homie) at a community play rehearsal. I love theater, so I decided to join a summer musical, *Beauty and the Beast*, even though I was still recovering mentally and physically from my brain injury. I used a walker at the time, and my anxiety was flowing through me because there were a bunch of younger divas running around. I remember feeling very uncomfortable until I saw another teenager closer to my age who walked up to me. Her mannerism was so genuine: "Hey, I'm Sophia," she said as she reached out her hand. Those three words changed my life. Needless to say, we started talking, and I felt much better. I never actually finished the play because the timing was not right for me. Despite this, my mom made sure I kept in contact with Sophia, who also attends the same church as me. She modeled in my fashion-show fundraiser that summer.

In October of 2012, she started volunteering for Riccio Pick-Me-Ups. She was inspired by the work we did in children's hospitals and aspired to be a child-life specialist. We have an awesomely authentic, mutual friend, Adrienne, who has been on many adventures with us as well. After a year of college in Alabama, Sophia switched to occupational therapy. She volunteered with me in an occupational therapy camp and saw how her grandma benefited from the therapy. Now she is on the path to becoming an occupational therapist.

We went through the journey of Granny (her grandma) fighting (and soon after passing away from) Alzheimer's[17] ("the beast") together. Spending time with Granny opened up more of my passions as well. Fast-forward years later, "O" becomes my best friend more and more each day. She was with me every step of the way as I slowly regressed from my illness in 2017. We both spent sick nights together, and we have shared many sleepovers, family conflicts, altruistic opportunities, and fun hangouts. She's my official personal assistant. Sophia used to transfer me, and she still provides tube feedings, exercises with me, and spends time just loving life with me. She is the person I tell secrets to and who sees me at my worst and best.

Whether it's holding my hand in the ER, calming my body on car rides, or soothing me to sleep, she is my outstanding "O." Sophia was the reason I reported a sexual assault that happened to me in a hospital. She knew something was wrong and encouraged me to share my inner voice to help other women who can be easily taken advantage of. One "silly girl" from *Beauty and the Beast* discovered her beautiful passion of becoming a therapist, and she advocated through the beasts of illnesses she had the courage to come in contact with.

A final note:

> Regardless of the experiences that shape us—good or bad—we always come out different on the other side. Pain often serves as its own catalyst for passion...fuel to the fire; purpose; drive. As you change, so too can your passions. They (and you) adapt like the laws of nature demand.
>
> The law of conservation of energy states that energy can neither be created or destroyed...just transformed. Think of yourself not as a passive object, but a force. (Jess)

What are some of your passions? Are they related to one another in some way? How do you use them in your life to make a difference?

Chapter 4
Education and Health

To know is one thing. To explore life (beyond the ledge) is another. Together, these things create knowledge.

KNOWLEDGE IS THE FUEL THAT drives the car of life. This knowledge is taught throughout one's lifetime. Everyone learns in a unique way—some quicker, others slower. Some might learn better visually, while others may learn better auditorily. Then there are tactile (through touch) learners, and kinesthetic (through movement) learners, and many can even learn through a unique mixture of ways.

Of course, most people have specific areas of interest: math, science, history, language arts, music, technology, psychology, etc. They focus on what they like in order to further their careers. However, the majority of people become most educated through experiences rather than from being in a classroom; education is not only defined by subjects learned in school but by the lessons that are taught in life.

There are people who, of course, have true passions for discovering something new. That seems to help the education process. Though regardless if passion is present, we can each learn the same lessons and take away something different. Every day is an opportunity to observe, to ask questions, and to learn lessons. These can be seen as blessings, no matter how positive or negative the situations might be.

(During my sophomore year of high school, I remember telling my mother that I didn't want to go to college. I was even afraid to take my psychology class during my junior year. But once I saw Kean, I knew I belonged. From there, I couldn't stop learning).

I have a passion to learn. On a cognitive or standardized test, however, my scores may be average to very low in some areas. How did I still get high honors in school? Well, what I realized was that studying through every life moment was the key. This opens the door to success, taking what was learned in the classroom and applying it to outside life. For example, in math, I tend to get distracted because its principles are so profound. During a lesson about infinite numbers, I struggled to focus because I thought of the infinity sign as it relates to love and dreamy possibilities. This simple math lesson got me thinking of so much more.

I know there are others like me. Anyone's mind can be drawn to certain subjects more than others. My strongest areas of educational interest are definitely creative arts, health, and psychology. Each of these is derived from science and humanities. I have personal experiences in the scope of health care, and these experiences aid me in the empathetic side of my studies. I can feel for both the patient and the professional. This is something I didn't learn in a classroom. I have met many other people who also use their personal health experiences as inspirations for their life missions, and most of the time, they're the most important life lessons they could have learned.

These personal experiences gave my education an entirely new context. What I thought I knew about health was blown into greater proportions when I attended college. I learned about so many theories, policies, professionals, and practices that I never knew existed. Everything I initially knew about health was from illness, injury, and disease. In school, I learned the greater picture and acquired a new outlook of what a person is made of.

According to the World Health Organization,[18] "Health is not merely the absence of disease," but a state of well-being within an individual as a whole. This includes six main domains:

- **Physical:** The parts of the body and brain, and our genetic makeup.

- **Psychological:** How we feel and express emotions; reason for actions.
- **Social:** The connection we have with others in the world, how we interact with people, and the strength of our relationships with family and friends.
- **Intellectual:** Thought processes, creativity, reasoning, judgment, and ways of learning.
- **Spiritual:** Includes a set of values, morals, and principles that guide our lives, not only through religion, but through an overall understanding for purpose and connection to the earth and beings.
- **Environmental:** The atmosphere we live in—air, water, living conditions, accessibility, economic status, and people around us.

All these factors influence the collective well-being. The struggle is maintaining balance and harmony in all areas. If one area is weak, other dimensions can compensate for it, bringing overall health. For example, I have met many individuals who have serious illnesses but have great overall health through radiating spiritual, social, and environmental dimensions. Every sensation, action, and activity affect different dimensions of ourselves. As a result, recreation and leisure are highly related to health. (More to be discussed in Part 3: Nourish).

My deep sadness in the past has created my happiness in
    the present
All the pain I had, and still endure, allows me to feel
    pleasant
That is OK if I am physically unstable
Asymmetrical in my thoughts and actions, I am still able
To find peace from stress
Become clean during a mess
Turn disappointments into satisfaction
And laziness into action
Feeling so tired yet wide awake
I give so much that I'll happily take

Take my life but not for granted
For I know I must bloom where I was planted

Although most people do not retain everything they learn, like my mom always says, "Knowledge is never wasted." Some people discover education and health more than others simply through experience. Before college, I was oblivious to how these two subjects were related. In reality, an increase in education increases health because individuals are more likely to be autonomous (take control) and access helpful resources to better themselves and others.

Mental health is more acknowledged now than it has been in the past, but it is still stigmatized compared to other aspects of health. The truth is, before acquiring my rare disease, which resulted in a severe physical disability, I felt mentally worse. My traumatic brain injury was primarily invisible. I looked normal to the eye and only appeared to act or move weirdly when you really spent some time with me. I was just so grateful to be alive. I hid my problems and propelled myself to my limits like many people do. Even though much of my condition is visible, the most bothersome parts are invisible: my tongue and autonomic nervous system.[19]

Amara on her thirteenth birthday, 2008

Did You Know?
According to the Invisible Disabilities Association,

74% of Americans who live with a severe disability do not use such devices [as a wheelchair]. Therefore, a disability cannot be determined solely by whether or not a person uses assistive equipment. The term we define invisible disability *refers to symptoms such as debilitating pain, fatigue, dizziness, cognitive dysfunctions, brain injuries, learning differences and mental health disorders, as well as hearing and vision impairments. These are not always obvious to the onlooker, but can sometimes or always limit daily activities, range from mild challenges to severe limitations, and vary from person to person.*[20]

Medical professionals often dismiss people for their genuine being if they have a history of anxiety, depression, or other mental illnesses. Also, the majority of people with severe chronic medical conditions, especially if they're rare, are blamed for being a victim of something purely psychological. Even if someone's condition is not organically medical, it still needs to be taken seriously—in many cases more seriously. Chronic medical conditions and mental illnesses have such a strong correlation that it is so often overlooked. Of course, a person is likely to be depressed and anxious when he or she has undergone trauma, pain, deteriorating abilities, or uncomfortable experiences all the time. Sometimes it becomes so severe that the psychiatric component must be addressed along with the physical.

Sometimes the most book-smart people often lack compassion and common sense. When I had a setback after my accident and acquired complex regional pain syndrome (CRPS),[21] I suppressed my feelings so that it seemed I was okay. My parents knew I was not okay because of the huge sign that indicated a lack of interest in things I normally enjoyed. I just wanted to be alone. A psychiatrist told my mom, "If we give her an antidepressant, that's like giving an alcoholic alcohol." I still do not know what that means. Well, in this case, an antidepressant, along with therapy, made a huge difference. My mood increased back to its normal level, and I started to progress and feel like myself again. Contrarily, my most recent illness was blamed on my previous conditions (when I was actively treating my mental health).

Since I was in middle school, I was struck to the core by the treatment of people with mental illnesses every time I visited my brother Lawrence in a pediatric psychiatric inpatient facility. His behaviors would often escalate when he had a physical problem, such as tooth pain. The psychiatric medicines sometimes caused other medical problems, like all medicines do. Unfortunately, physical, emotional, and sexual abuse in health care and disability settings are all too real, as I have experienced.

As you can see, I can rant endlessly about health care incompetence and the problems with control by insurance and pharmaceutical companies that truly mess with millions of peoples' lives. Errors in health care are a LEADING cause of death and injury.[22] All scientists, including doctors, have hypotheses based on evidence that is proven wrong again and again. That is how they continue to learn, and the field of medicine grows.

This section was the most difficult because I aim to accurately raise awareness and empathize for those facing rare and undiagnosed illnesses like myself. I have always been an advocate for people with disabilities and chronic illnesses since my brain injury, but only now do I truly understand the struggle. The brain is truly the most mysterious and vital organ, making neurology a really difficult area of practice. Receiving a diagnosis that indicates a serious disorder is devastating. Having a serious condition that is misdiagnosed and undiagnosed can be even more devastating.

Although I am no longer surprised, I cringe every time I read about someone who was not believed or was misdiagnosed because of complexities of a rare disease, systemic illness, incompetent professionals, genetic involvement, or testing inaccuracy. From my experiences, conditions that do not have an underlying structural barrier are overlooked. Special tests are needed to look at muscle, nerve, arterial, and specific immune functions. Additionally, I noticed a major change in compassionate care from pediatrics to adulthood. Women and young adults are often stereotyped for either being too stressed or wanting drugs, which does happen as well.

We are all hanging in there—hanging on to hope that we will soon swing and climb. I did have my pull-up, then I was pulled down by a mystery—a mystery that is solved by my theoretical formula: D.A.N.C.E. Honestly, sometimes when someone asks, "How do you feel?" I say, "Well..." and laugh because I do not know what else to say. I have no idea why I am feeling this way, and professionals say they cannot do anything to help. I'm living on theories of what has possibly happened and what is currently happening to me. I say "Well" because of these frustrations of losing control of muscles (but I can control my wellness!). This lack of control is still tough to swallow and a real jerk (myoclonus[23]). My mind twists and turns more than my uncontrollable body at times. Despite all this, my education, faith, and support system teach me I have been given chances to share my dances.

Did You Know?[24]

- *In the United States, a condition is considered rare if it affects fewer than 200,000 people.*
- *There are about 7,000 known rare diseases in the United States, with more to be discovered.*
- *About 30 million people in the United States have been diagnosed with a rare disease.*
- *Many are life-threatening, and more than 90 percent (as of 2019) do not have FDA-approved treatment.*
- *It takes an average of eight years to receive an accurate diagnosis of a rare disease, as initial misdiagnoses are common.*

Rare Disease Day: (February 28, 2020)

I have been celebrating this awareness day for five years. Each year, I approach the day with more education, passion, and thoughts. I am so proud of our friends at Fighting H.A.R.D. (Have a Rare

Disease) Foundation for shining a light on this cause and bringing Rare Your Genes programs to Monmouth and Ocean County areas while helping Rare families.

A huge part of having a rare disease is finding a correct diagnosis, which many times is not even found until after an autopsy. I am on this journey, which doctors two years ago at Downstate Hospital cautioned us would be one of no answers or treatment. They knew my condition would get worse over time. We are still fighting, and I'm still breathing; I am still me, just without controlled voice and mobility. I will update on my health another day. For now, I wanted to share a song I wrote this week. Music and meditation are my life these days.

Background

I heard the classic tale of "The Ugly Duckling" from my *Calm* app and felt a deep relatability.

- SWAN: Syndrome Without a Name—especially unknown genetic disorders in children.
- Zebra: A symbol for those with rare diseases.
- Unicorns: They don't exist yet. We believe in their beauty and magic, so they are real.

People may say we should just die (I overheard staff at a hospital referring to me) or that it doesn't matter. Every life DOES matter.

Live on, swanacorn: ode to the rare.

Swanacorn

Who are you to say who I am?
I'm me now and some of them
What does it mean to be them?
The ugly duckling
Been through such suffering

It lived being told lies
Bird so beautiful…he swims and flies
Did you know he was ready to die?
Until a teared reflection showed it was a swan
This story of truth lives on…and on…

Uhh-gly means uhh…you don't know me
Not the value of beauty…ooh
We love you oodles and oodles
Care for the rare
Live on, swan
Swim and fly; this is not goodbye
Live on and on

Because the hoofprint can be a mix of black and white
Maybe a zebra with colored stripes
Or believe it can be a unicorn dancing tonight

Uhh-gly means uhh…you don't know me
Not the value of beauty…ooh

We love you oodles and oodles
Care for the rare
Live on, zebra
Dare to dance—this your chance
Live on, unicorn

It can be sickening
It can be scary and really hurt
But every being has wondrous worth
You are more than a word
To the strange, speechless bird…you deserve to be heard

Uhh-gly means uhh…you don't know me
Not the value of beauty…ooh
We love you oodles and oodles

Care for the rare
Odd ducks; offbeat horses
Not asking who, why, and where
We love you…ooh
Live on, swanacorn…

I have had the honor of increasing my education outside of school by volunteering, when I met many zebras and swanacorns. In 2016, I met two intelligent, compassionate, and courageous sisters (Allie and Jonna) during their hospital stays. Allie lived with chronic illnesses all her life, then Jonna developed severe gastroparesis[25] at age ten, finally receiving an experimental gastric pacemaker[26] at age thirteen, which helped her to eat once again. These girls and their amazing parents started the Fighting H.A.R.D. Foundation to show support for the millions who do not have a foundation for supporting and researching their illnesses (see Resources).

Are you healthy? Educated? How do you define that, and how have experiences in the health and education fields helped you grow as a person? Break it up into domains. You may surprise yourself. Did you learn anything new from this chapter?

Chapter 5
Unseen Magic

When we think back to our mystified curiosities for magic; anything special and out of the ordinary that seems impossible; amazing; entertaining; something not just everyone can do... We are in awe of the imagined capabilities of the human being. If only we were flowing with power and able to make miracles, or just make ourselves fly. If only we could do something moving; something not everyone else can do; something that takes particular ability and is absolutely fascinating all the same. Though, are talents not like magic? These capabilities we call skills, which never cease to amaze, surprise, create envy, awe, and inspire? This music we make; the lengths we jump; the melodies we sing; the thoughts we put into words; the masterpieces we build; the way our bodies move in synchronization; the creations not everyone can do. They're like superpowers... They are gifts. We are wizards.

—Jessica Giannone

I HAVE ALWAYS BEEN A believer in magic. To this day, I still become excited thinking about mermaids, unicorns, fairies, and princesses. I am astonished by watching magic acts. I've even dreamed of dating a magician (but then I realized they would always be disappearing). This chapter describes the magic of the invisible forces we experience every day: hope, faith, and love.

On June 3, 2008, while I was still in a coma in the pediatric intensive care unit, a handsome young man walked through the hospital doors. His name was James. He sustained a similar brain injury from a car accident two months prior. My parents called James their angel, as he gave hope that I, too, could receive a miracle. My mom is now good friends with his mom, and I occasionally hang out with James. Each time we reunite, we're reminded of the miracle that connected us.

Throughout the years of recovery from my brain injury, I found out what hope was to me. I wrote the following poem in 2016 (revised from a poem I wrote in 2012):

Hope

Dark clouds cover my mind
With more clouds coming from behind
But when the sky looks grim
There's a ray of light I feel from within
It can be in the form of a butterfly, rainbow, or just love
    from a friend
This seems like magic from fictional fairies using periwin-
    kle pixie dust
But it comes from something greater; a unique spiritual
    trust
Helps reach into all that is possible and deny those thoughts
    of what can't be probable
Even if the thoughts are hibernating in my cheerless, clut-
    ter-filled brain
I see symbols and signs that take away the pain
Love and support from others make me feel protected and
    connected
Allowing myself to be that little peak
Between the darkness and light that many often seek
These everyday miracles are why I believe
That in people, places, or things, this magic will conceive
Bringing HOPE and giving it to others as a lift

To cherish our presence, HOPE will be the ribbon to fully help unwrap our gift

What are some things that bring you hope? Do certain people in your life give you hope? Some examples may be children, animals, nature, or anything that reminds you of the possibilities of the future. Besides butterflies, flowers, and singing birds, listening to music gives me hope. The positive vibrations, unique melodies, and moving lyrics make me feel so alive. I feel connected to a song, which makes me feel less alone. (If you want to listen to a variety of hope, faith, and love music tracks, on *Spotify*, I created a playlist: "This is Why I DANCE.")

Faith gives people hope. Regardless of religion, a strong faith typically correlates with a strong sense of love. Although I was raised as a Catholic and still practice Catholicism, my beliefs are more open than those of my religion. Some spiritual practices of the eastern world that I'm interested in, such as yoga and meditation, are actually becoming more mainstream. They are guided specifically by Buddhism, but I feel most religions have the same positive messages. They help guide our values, morals, and beliefs.

Spirituality differs from religion because it's about finding a greater, individual purpose, free from any religious dogmas. Famous author and researcher Brenè Brown describes spirituality as "recognizing and celebrating that we are all inextricably connected to each other by a power greater than all of us...grounded in love and compassion."[27]

Faith helps me strengthen my spiritual spine with God as my backbone. It awakens the free, kindred, and enlightened spirit, creating magic and miracles. Miracles are not seen in a mirror but summoned from secret reflection, introspection, and perception. I believe in the everyday miracles that happen, such as the "almost/ so close" moments, which I now deem "Amaracles" (see chapter 22, "Mirror Calls" song).

Faith

Faith is the magic that helps turn death into life
Creates happiness from strife
Unseen and unheard by us now
But our history makes us say "Wow"

It's not just what was said to happen in the past
Faith of all kinds is sometimes such that will forever last
Whatever higher power one believes
It's the invisible magic within that conceives

Miracles are things that skepticism cannot overpower
For faith is the extra sunlight and water that grows life's
flower

In March of 2016, I met fellow beautiful brain injury survivor Cristabelle Braden at a Brain Injury Alliance of New Jersey gala, where she sang inspiring songs about hope. I was so excited to connect with this creative and courageous young woman. We kept in contact, but since she lived two hours away in Pennsylvania, I did not see her again until I was in an inpatient rehabilitation facility in Allentown, Pennsylvania. Cristabelle came about six times to sing and hang out with me. I had trouble speaking, yet when she played her songs, I started to sing multiple phrases at a time.

Prior to this, I had not sung since early fall before my voice became dysphonic.[28] Together we sang, improvised, and just prayed. She even brought her cat to visit me!

Dare to hope again...dare to pray for miracles that I can't comprehend...take the leap of faith. (Cristabelle Braden)

I felt the Lord's presence in those moments, giving me faith that everything would be OK through all the therapies, confusion, and illness. Cristabelle even told me she was supposed to be in Nashville at the time. In 2020, I found out she was in a very dark place emotionally during the time I was at Good Shepherd Rehabilitation. I certainly believe we brought each other needed hope.

Cristabelle has released wonderful new albums and a podcast called *Declaration Life* with a motto: "Declare your purpose. Declare your place. Declare your worth." I feel deeply connected to her messages, voice, and soul. Experiences and people like Cristabelle make me believe that maybe there truly is a reason for everything. I think we all have seasons where our hope has diminished, yet faith and love keep hope alive.

Faith and love indeed have a correlation. I learned God is love. He created all we know to love. So seriously, what is love? I think it's different for everyone. It's such a powerful emotion, force, and entity with countless songs, movies, and books about it. Our world lives on love; not just because of procreation-type love, but also because of the kindness we give to each other.

All our sensations help us generate this feeling. I do think of it as an emotion, but it can be a noun, adjective, and verb as well. Love is love is love is LOVE. We all need it and yearn for it. In my opinion, love is **L**istening, **O**pening, **V**alidating, and **E**xperiencing. Sadly, there are some barriers for people to find love in people and things—barriers based on sexuality, gender, religion, and disabilities.

The truth is, at almost twenty-five years old, I had never yet kissed anyone or had a real date, yet I still feel an abundance of love all the time from my friends, family, and those around me. I mean, there was a self-proclaimed bad boy yogi who shut the door in my face on my only casual date night. There was my Latino high school crush from junior physics class who broke promises and eventually ghosted me (repeatedly not returning messages). I realized that just as my personality and illness is undefined, so is my sexuality: rainbow pride. I'm not sugarcoating how sweet love is. Let's just say it's the icing on the cake that warms the cold and battered.

All my lovely puns aside, when I was eight, I wrote a poem saying, "Beauty is everywhere; every person, place, and thing." Beauty is found because of love. Love is everywhere, radiating inside out, just like beauty. As the classic phrase goes, "beauty is in the eye of the beholder." What beholds our hearts may surprise us. Hearts symbolize love. If we feel love from our brains, why is the symbol a heart?

The chambers of the heart pump blood to the
brain
So we can function and stay sane
Blood so red, vital, and pure
For many transfusing, it is the only cure

It works from the heart
Which can be broken apart
Departing…and clotting as you lose
More love is needed to heal the deep bruise

We feel it beat from our chest
Our "dancing lifeline," to say it best
"Lub dub lub" is its typical sound
One heart to another, it goes around

Thank you, God, for hope, faith, and love giving
us another day
Another day
To pray, to play
To say thank you
For waking up and feeling OK
Another day of feeling love
Guided from my angels above

Sometimes I feel like it's just another day—same struggles, same story—waiting and fighting. The truth is, some things stay the same. But things are always changing. Each day we prepare for the next. Each day is magic because we are here to experience it. Some days there's a morsel, and other days there's an abundance. It's the awe in some: *awesome* magic makes us D.A.N.C.E.!

I realized my subconscious never spews so much out into the real world as it does when I'm writing. I can see it. It's in tangible form. My fingers are literally connecting with the gateway to the world as my brain controls the instruments—it's used to implement the shattering of a barrier...between my mind and everyone else. You see it. You feel it. It is now yours. (Jessica Giannone)

*Are you strong in your faith and/or spirituality? How does this help strengthen your ability to love life seeing invisible magic each day?

Chapter 6
Discover Yourself

To ask myself "Who am I?" what a question this will be
I ask myself not who I am, but who I think I'll be
Looking in to see what we'll be is the closest we are to "now"
But I cannot answer "Who am I?" because I don't know how
How can we define a thing that questions itself to be?
I can say the things I like, but that does not say me
I can tell you what I think I know and show you where I've been
But I cannot be certain of the truths that lie within
—Excerpt of "Who Am I?" poem by Jessica Giannone

WHO I AM TODAY MAY be different than who I was yesterday and who I will be tomorrow. One of the greatest parts of life is that all of us creatures evolve over time. Some things stay more constant in certain people throughout their lives than in others. I feel like I am much of the same person personality-wise that I was since I was a young girl. In contrast, experiences, education, and natural life development will help shape who I am in the future. At this time, I could think of who

I want to be and try to become that person. In reality, I have many morals, ethics, and ideas that may change.

Before my accident, I thought my physical abilities were the biggest part of who I was. People knew me for my dancing and tumbling skills. It took me a couple of years to realize they were a part of me, yet I have so much more inside. Finding oneself is really difficult, and it's even harder when one's life is unexpectedly changed by an illness, injury, or tragedy. Although "Discover" is the first part of D.A.N.C.E., it takes the entire process to cycle a few rounds before fully discovering the self. Finding out who the people, places, and things around us are, along with diversity, education, health, and the invisible forces that keep us moving, will continue every day. Some may say life's a mystery, but imagine you're the detective and find out all you can. We can all solve it in our own ways. The treasure is the well-being, joy, and enjoyable moments. So let's continue in figuring out our own beats to this D.A.N.C.E.

Selfie (March 19, 2018)

We live in a selfie world. Yes, many people might be too self-absorbed, but part of developing as a human is finding and creating yourself. During the last semester of my graduate school human development class, I learned how toddlers recognize the concept of the self and how that concept expands and changes throughout our life spans, developmentally and situationally. People have always told me how helping and loving others start from focusing on oneself. Well, focusing on oneself (especially in regard to health) can be daunting. During this entire process, I feel like I am too self-involved because of my condition. Despite this, I still try to be emotionally supportive to others. Faith helps to remind me that there's so much more than myself.

Yesterday I took a selfie with help from my occupational therapist for shoulders and hands. It made me contemplate myself, and I hope that it helps you too. It's difficult to describe my progress and how I feel. I am never in it to win it (which is controversial); I am in it just to dance with 100 percent of myself.

I am always learning about the self.

Acceptance: I am me in whatever state I am in; I am here.

Advocacy: Can I try? Is this an option? I just need some assistance on…(Mom is there for me too, but I am becoming more assertive in adult life).

Awareness: I know my strengths and limitations (unlike with my acute TBI).

Blame: Why did I do that? It's my fault.

Care: Necessary to function. It's emotional, social, spiritual, cognitive, and physical.

Confidence: I am me. This is what I enjoy, stand for, believe, think, and feel (developed in my young adult years).

Control: What move should I make? Do I have time to think and focus? Is my brain just going to go?

Criticism: I could have done so much better. Why do I make these choices? How can I be so messed up?

Doubt: Will I really be able to beat something that's not in my power? Am I living in a fantasy?

Efficacy: I believe I can achieve.

Gratification: I am so proud of all my accomplishments; it makes me so happy.

Harm: I can so easily hurt myself to a point where it scares me (my intentions are not to harm, so if possible, I think of risk).

Healing: Art, music, dance, and spirituality are the best medicines for me.

Image: Image fluctuates with my changing body, but my persona of a natural, artsy flower child takes over.

Love: I mean… I give it to others, so you know, I love me too.

Motivation: I got this! I need to do this for all the people and things I love in life.

Pity: Ugh, I hate this one, but sometimes my "Why not?" says "Why me?" I learned to have a quick pity party, cry, then suck it up and enjoy it the best I can.

Respect: I am worth as much as you are, so I am not going to lessen myself because of the circumstances I am dealing with.

Realization: This is why I am who I am. I remember… I think I can improve.

Regulation: I need to monitor my thoughts, feelings, and even breaths to lessen stimulation.

Sacrifice: It's my choice to help make life easier and more rewarding, even if I lose out on comfort, joy, or benefits. It's so worth it.

Support: How can I be as helpful as possible with people taking care of all my needs? Physically, I am dependent, but emotionally, can I support myself and others? YES.

Each new discovery in life helps us unearth ourselves more and more.

I am 85 years old, and I still don't know what I want to be when I grow up. (Uncle Jimmy Genovese)

It can be so overwhelming when we self-contemplate and cause anxiety. From elementary school children to graduate school adults, when asked the big question ("Who are you?"), most people freeze up in confusion, fright, or panic. Every time I think I know who I am, life keeps reminding me there's so much more.

I Am (February 5, 2018)

One of the greatest gifts from my cousin Jessica was an art kit to create an "I Am" poster.

I am the woman I was destined to be
I am more than the complexities inside me
I am finally surrounded by people who care
I am learning to accept that I am rare

Being in a teaching hospital feels amazing! I can connect to the medical students and learn with them. I was evaluated by therapy, and I will have to try to get myself moving and decrease atrophy[29] during this time. Not many results today! Whatever this is, it is a serious, complicated, and long process, but I am READY.

I am breathing, which I need to work on because any muscle movement is causing more spasms and complications, including not being able to talk as much. I am going to try to get more sleep tonight.

I am once again thankful for my parents and loved ones, including my cousin Jessica, who gave me the "I Am" empowerment poster, which my mom helped me with today. Now the health professionals can just look at the poster and know who I am. I keep telling myself I am strong, even when I feel otherwise. Tomorrow's a new day to be who you are!

> *What we think we want and what is actually "right" for us may still be changing, and that means we're living free from the bounds of some present, unyielding narrative. This is a blessing. (Jessica Giannone)*

*With all that said, who are you?

Part 2
Accomplish

Accomplish: to bring to completion; to succeed in reaching.[30]
Achieving is what keeps me believing, just
as believing keeps me achieving.

Success happens in those who fail
Just how strength is found most in those who are frail
These contradictions speak true
Just as the old becomes new
No better feeling than saying "now I can…"
Do it; do anything; true power of man and woman

WHAT DO YOU THINK OF when you hear the words *accomplish* and *achieve*? Is victory measured by the number of awards and recognitions one receives? First place means it's always the best, right? I guess sometimes it does, but it does not mean the triumph is of any greater value than someone else's victory. For example, a teenager who walks for the first time after a serious injury may be valued as being as strong as someone receiving an Olympic medal. One student can get a B for a grade and feel so proud, and another may get an A and be indifferent toward it. For someone with a mental illness, just waking up, going to work, and doing his or her best at daily activities can be an accomplishment. Every achievement is customized to one's abilities and lifestyle. In this world where everything seems to be a competition, we must remember the only true competitor is yourself.

In sixth grade, I wrote an essay stating that my biggest challenge was to be the best I could be. More than a decade later, it's still my greatest obstacle, which can be empathized with for most individuals. Each small achievement leads to a larger one. There is always room for improvement, even after the mastery of a skill, because butterflies of life exist; change happens. Hard work, dedication, determination, confidence, and resilience help lead to achieving goals, regardless of size.

Some goals are precisely set in the mind or even written down. Other goals can be achieved without even consciously realizing they were goals. Each goal leads to another, which helps show that dreams do come true. There's no age limit for reaching for your goals and dreams. Some people start at three; others at eighty-three. Realistically, not every goal we set for ourselves is achieved. Fortunately, life can take you on a U-turn, leading to another path on a highway full of other achievements. Accomplishments are the factors that enhance the D.A.N.C.E.; they keep the rhythm going.

Amara graduates from Kean University, May 2017

Chapter 7
Confidence and Resilience

The ability to jump with joy, feeling like a champion, is ordinarily awesome; but to bounce back with that same warrior spirit is extraordinarily amazing.

Amara trying to catch up with her brother and little cousin at a family barbecue, September 2015

WHEN I WAS PONDERING IDEAS for this book, my brother Robert suggested I write this chapter. He says that confidence and resilience are two forces needed to achieve something. In my mind, confidence is believing that you can do it; whatever the "it" can be. It's believing that you are amazing, but also that others have the same power to be incredible too. (This is, of course, different from someone who is conceited, someone who thinks he or she is better than everyone else.

If a person thinks this all the time, that person might be a narcissist.) Narcissistic individuals can still be successful, but they will surely hurt others in the process and ultimately push away those who would be most important to them.

Confidence is a trait that I was born with to some degree. I always felt confident when performing in front of others, while being me was still difficult. Similarly, many tweens and teens can relate to having distorted ideals that they are not as pretty, smart, kind, funny, or worthy as other people who are popular. Despite the love that myself and many other children I've met have received, I still felt these negative feelings. Although bullying is definitely a factor in lack of confidence, I think in some ways it can build confidence. Something that you were made fun of for may very well be the quirk that makes you realize how interesting you truly are and how much you can stand out from the crowd. Withstanding the insignificant snickers makes you all the more bold.

Adversity is the bridge to evolution. (Jessica Giannone)

A couple of years after my accident, I learned that being silly, weird, and doing what made me happy was what others laughed at. Gradually, throughout the years, I switched my perception and became even more Amara to make people laugh. Now I laugh at myself and laugh with people. This helps others know they can be themselves too. Confidence in myself continues to help me in everything I do. It lets me grow like a tree, allowing me to branch out to new experiences and expand my abilities, leading me to the next magical force of achievement: resilience.

Resilience is the way a person can get up after being knocked down. It is a trait seen in the most famous, intelligent, and successful people. It's about having that "never give up" attitude. Being resilient helps with being confident, and confidence gives you the power to be resilient.

Real accomplishments do not happen easily—not on the first try. The determination to keep going after disappointments, failures, and difficult situations is what makes someone a true champion.

There were a multitude of moments and months when I was down-and-out. I did not believe in the beauty of the future. I saw no light. In relation to many, I was struggling with depression and mental illness. This did not display weakness, but it showed my strength. It truly exposed the resiliency and confidence I gained on my journey back to me. Like a lot of us, I was figuring it all out. New circumstances occurred, and go figure that I'm still figuring it out.

Learning to cope with my various challenges helped me believe that I could be a champion. I saw children much younger than myself dealing with more severe conditions and still living life to the fullest. These youngsters were, and still are, my heroes. They are like rocks because they don't seem to break. However, rocks do break down. It's called erosion. Though erosion can be powerful and life-changing, it ends up creating the most unique and beautiful land formations.

Life is like a mountain. It can be beautifully breathtaking, or it can be intimidating and scary, depending on where you are and how you look at it. It takes many forms and serves many roles. Stand at the top, and you've conquered the world...overlooking the remarkable scenes your surroundings have to offer, feeling like you've accomplished it all. Stand at the bottom, and you realize how high that sharp, rugged, and deathly rock actually is, and it seems impossible to reach the top. Sometimes there are shortcuts. You don't always have to risk it all clambering up the cliff, but sometimes you do. Sometimes you pass gracefully flowing streams and admire the flowers swaying tall through the wind, or you sneak onto an off-beaten path leading you to a trail you never knew existed. Whether you get there or not, you will run into obstacles, and you will face unexpected adventures, serene perspectives. It can be terrifying, and it can be sweet, wondrous. Just like a mountain...with anything, there comes bad and good. Either way, you have to look to the sun. (Jessica Giannone)

It's good to break down once in a while. Emotions are a part of life. Besides, how do we rock without rolling down? The achievement of our beautiful life force comes from the erosion. We are still rocks, just in different forms—always being molded, still solid, yet always rolling along.

Rock Star

Rocks are below, stars are above
They form because of love
We need the rocks to climb to a star
Just as humans must face challenges to find who they are
The ones who do with grace and a smile
Well, they are rock stars in style
Making music to their own beats
Rock stars are the everyday elite!

Warriors fight individual battles of bigger fights. Examples of those struggles can be mental disorders, physical disabilities, terminal illnesses, drugs, abuse, poverty, and so much more. Here are powerful song lyrics from my friend Cristabelle Braden's new album, *Declaration.*

I am a different kind of warrior…you might not see me fight, but I know I am victorious each day that I survive… Even if nobody sees it, I choose to believe that my story is not over… I'm a different kind of warrior.[31]

Warriors

Warriors come in all different shapes and sizes
Different atmospheres and surprises
It takes a loss for a win

But no matter what, these champions grin
Every day, look for that warrior of motivation
You, too, can be that inspiration
Sometimes it's the most complex stories
That lead to the greatest of glories
Here or there, circle or square
A hero is a hero anywhere

Believing that you are a champion helps enhance your super-power: CONFIDENCE, allowing you to dance in the face of adversity—RESILIENCE.

Heroes

Whether you're on the front, side, back, inside, or outside of the lines during a crisis, we all have the power to be a hero, even on a typical day. All occupations and people are essential to someone somewhere. Although recognition should not be motivation, receiving authentic words of appreciation is reciprocated with extreme gratitude and joy.

Below is a *Facebook* post from my father during the COVID-19 pandemic (April 11, 2020):

> It was much easier to be a hero before the pandemic. Today, our heroes face danger helping COVID patients and are exposed to a deadly virus. We all need to pray and ask God for his saving grace.
>
> The dispensation of more than chemotherapy.
>
> I was walking down the hall at the end of my shift as an oncology pharmacist at the Brooklyn VA Medical Center on Holy Thursday in the year of 2004. Walking toward me was the daughter of one of my patients who had been

receiving regular treatments as an outpatient for AML leukemia.[32] I had become friendly with Mr. A and his family as I have done with many other patients and their families, as these people receive regularly scheduled treatments for relatively long periods of time. As she was walking toward me, I could sense her sadness and emotional turmoil, and it reminded me [of] the way I felt, like heavy dark clouds pressing down on my head and shoulders when I left my mother in the ICU the night before she died, succumbing to cholangiocarcinoma.[33] Of course, I asked the obvious question, for which I knew the answer: "How's Dad doing?" In a tearful voice, she replied, "Dad's very sick, and I think he's dying." I then hugged her firmly, and she cried on my shoulder. I left that night teary-eyed, thinking, "What could I do for this family?"

On the way home to Staten Island, I decided to stop at the fruit and vegetable store in Brooklyn and pick up apples and other fruit, remembering that Mr. A said he liked apples. When I got home, I asked my wife for a basket and told her my plan. We arranged the fruit in the basket along with prayers, angels, and an inspirational poem that my daughter Amara wrote.

On Saturday morning, I decided that we would drop off the basket, and my daughter and I went up to the eighth floor oncology inpatient unit to hand the basket to Mr. A and his family. The patient was surrounded by 10 to 12 family members, and we found out that he went into a coma the day before. The family was very appreciative [of] the basket, and Amara and I told them that we would pray for Mr. A.

On Monday, Mr. A passed away. I received a card from his daughter later in the week thanking me for the basket and prayers and informing me that her father woke from his coma on Easter Sunday, stuck his hand in the basket, and pulled out and ate an apple. She said her dad was alert and interactive the whole day and that the family was thankful that they had some closure.

I wasn't sure what I wanted for the family when I made the basket, but then I realized that this [was] what I was really praying for. A month later, Mr. A's daughter, who worked for a large charity, did a presentation at my son and daughter's grade school, and she called the names of my children to come up on stage. My kids were so excited to tell me about what happened at school that day, and I felt something I never felt before. I felt like a hero.

Inspiration[34]

"a: divine influence or action on a person believed to qualify him or
  her to receive and communicate sacred revelation"
"b: the action or power of moving the intellect or emotions"
"c: the act of influencing or suggesting opinions"

"You are an inspiration." This phrase can be the most meaningful or meaningless, depending on the context and person saying it. People with disabilities are often called inspirations solely for that purpose alone. We just choose to live, and yeah, of course we all have the ability to achieve something. I appreciate when people are inspired by me if it changed something about their lives. I know my teen volunteers have written in college essays that I inspired them to be confident and resilient along with inspiring their career choices because of how I chose to live my life.

Personally, I am inspired by almost everything. I think I draw much of my inspiration from nature and faith. Obviously, my family, friends, and life circumstances in themselves inspire me; they all led me to my D.A.N.C.E. Each individual I meet or new place I go to ripples the waves of my actions. When people, including millions of children, face unbelievable challenges in life, I'm inspired to believe—believe that there must be a reason for this, believe in community, believe in miracles, believe I can be part of that circle. I'm an adult child living openly because of a community, a unity. The South African word *Ubuntu* encompasses this: "I am because we are."

Additionally, my past actions—even the most embarrassing ones—inspired my path for the future. People I have worked with inspired me every day because I always learned something new from them. I'm inspired by the power of communication: those who speak loud and proud yet use no words and people who move despite limited movement. There are both historical and living individuals whom I admire for different aspects of their journeys, from civil rights activists, artists, and entertainers to saints. There are way too many to name. As far as using writing, imagination, and play to convey empowering messages, Dr. Seuss (Theodor Seuss Geisel) is one of my top favorites.

Here are some Seussy selections:

> *In my world, everyone's a pony and they all eat rainbows and poop butterflies!*

> *From there to here, from here to there, funny things are everywhere!*

> *I'm sorry to say so but, sadly, it's true that Bang-ups and Hang-ups can happen to you.*

> *Today you are you! That is truer than true! There is no one alive who is you-er than you!*

Be who you are and say what you feel, because those who mind don't matter, and those who matter don't mind. (Commonly attributed to Dr. Seuss, but the expression has been linked to numerous sources since the 1930s.)

Don't cry because it's over, smile because it happened. (Commonly attributed to Dr. Seuss, but a form of the saying is traced back to German poet Ludwig Jacobowski in 1899.)

We're all a little weird. And life is a little weird. And when we find someone whose weirdness is compatible with ours, we join up with them and fall into mutually satisfying weirdness—and call it love— true love." (Robert Fulghum, commonly attributed)

Everyone and everything in this book I mention genuinely inspires me.

*Who truly inspires (or has inspired) you to be confident, resilient, and achieve your best life? This isn't just someone you might admire, but someone who set a match in your soul to ignite change, altering or creating a beginning to something in your life.

Chapter 8
Everyday Achievements

Your accomplishment is measured not by the quality of the triumph itself, but by the quantity of effort you put into completing it.

I may be a little lazy, but when I set my mind to a project, I grind and get it done. I'm a highly successful businessman... It's all or nothing. (Uncle Neil Giannone)

I HAVE FELT THE GREATEST pride doing tasks I have previously struggled to do. Having a conversation with my friend, with her understanding most of my ideas, was just a goal I worked toward daily. However, it was a huge achievement for me in my most recent neurological journey. If I can make a difference to someone every day, even if it's in a small way, such as making a person smile through a small deed or message, then I feel fulfilled. Writing this book an hour, half hour, or even five minutes a day is something I am proud of. It's an everyday achievement that leads to the bigger ones: dreams coming true.

In my last semester of college, I worked as a writing tutor. I realized for some people, including myself, the most difficult part is getting started. Sometimes it's harder to maintain or finish tasks, such as New Year's resolutions. The key is persistence against resistance.

It's those times you say "Yayyy"
"I just completed that today"
Whether it's an application
Or you found out important information
Finished the test
That you completed with your best
Effort, like just completing one chore
Or reminding yourself what you're here for
And when everything is going wrong
You keep going strong
Continuing with your plight
Not giving up your fight

As a child, I was named one of those overachievers because I pushed myself to my greatest capability. I do not think it was too much because I was happy as long as I did something. I did everything, and I still do—with love and with only those who I like and love. Due to my own experiences and observations, people with these types of overachiever personalities are more likely to stress out and develop illnesses (mental or physical), usually early on in life. Sometimes I exhibit perfectionist qualities, though I am an expressionist. I need to communicate and complete tasks based on how I feel.

The year after my accident when I had a setback, I felt jealous toward my brother Rob, who communicated, "You're so imperfect that you're perfect." I had anxiety trying to live up to expectations I thought people had of me to be "amazing." On the other hand, my brother was just himself—a fun-loving kid who made mistakes and didn't worry about pleasing others (so I thought). On the contrary, he was struggling with his own insecurities and peer pressure too, like most adolescents. Rob lives every day to the fullest, and I try to do the same in my own way. His constant socializing, which I have joked about, is helping him network and become successful in his career of communications!

In my situation, it's much more difficult to achieve everyday tasks, as I need setup and guidance to do so because of physical limitations. Once I am given the opportunity to accomplish a goal, I feel productive, which enhances my overall quality of life. I pray that everyone can have that support to achieve too. Maybe that's my mission: to help be a catalyst for others to feel and achieve things over the moon, overcoming challenges by using D.A.N.C.E. in everyday life. This is why I am an "overcat" and not an underdog (which my brother considers himself to be). Underdogs are the ones who rise to the occasion despite past circumstances or what others think. I believe it is even more so in the achievement of overcats; they surprise others with their unperfected purr-fection, curiosity, and methods of amazing accomplishments.

Wabi-Sabi (February 12, 2020)

Wabi-sabi is a new word I learned through daily meditation with my friend Brett. It's a Japanese philosophy meaning to embrace imperfection and impermanence of life.

Presently, my perspective and sight are narrow. My mind is open wide with colorful imagery. The neuro-ophthalmologist[35] confirmed several motor and nerve issues with my eyes. I knew surgery wouldn't be recommended because of my systematic CNS (central nervous system) involvement. We try because maybe...hope. I do need to see a neurologist because I need prescription refills, but all neurologists dismissed me. Pseudobulbar syndrome is going crazy.

I am writing this fully supported with at least seven pillows in a dark room, sitting up but also slouched in a hospital bed. My giant teddy bear and eye mask are covering my left eye, and I can see in the dark with my phone facing downward. So, as you know, I basically live in bed. If you told me that a year or two ago, I would have cried immensely. I miss being out in the community. When I do go in my wheelchair, I feel like a different person—extremely uncomfortable, uncontrolled, immobilized, and unable to communicate and appreciate.

Mindfulness has kept me grateful and breathing through this funky flow. I love doing art and music with my therapists. I've been dancing with my friends, and it's amazing. My home OT (occupational therapist) will help with my positioning issues in bed and in the chair. My cousin Jessica and I are serious about finishing our book. I want to be productive and make a difference as much as possible.

The idea of a purr-fect wabi-sabi life was demonstrated in my three-legged Bengal cat, beautiful Baboo. After almost fifteen years, he took his last breaths peacefully at home a couple of weeks ago. Until the very end, he communicated and made an effort to show himself, the neighborhood, my family, and me love. My other cats are too lazy to jump on my bed, though they run around the house, causing commotion. Yet my terminally ill and disabled Baboo tried with all his might even to his last day to get on my bed so he could cuddle with me. He is forever my Valentine.

Emotionally, it's overwhelming to hear and read about tragedies and deaths happening constantly. I know I just need to breathe and pray God will show all those suffering beautiful love.

Wabi-sabi, my beautiful loves.

Amara and Baboo, October 2009

Healing Marathon

In April 2016, I was asked to put together an awareness presentation for a sorority and my brother's fraternity. I had limited notice and needed it ready within a few hours. Somehow, I made sure my schoolwork was done so I could work on the presentation, which meant decreasing my nap time. It was one of those daily achievements that led to more than just another successful presentation. At the time, I was preparing for a sprint that led to a marathon that would, in turn, change my life without me even realizing it.

I ultimately met an extraordinary friend, Brett, whom I vaguely knew through another event, but this instance was the first time we talked. He opened up about his chronic illnesses, along with interests and other small talk. We exchanged numbers and slowly developed a special friendship built on encouragement, support, and just innocent, soulful love. He was hospitalized with a serious infection a year before I was. I felt helpless and simply tried to cheer him up with supportive messages the best I knew how. When I became sick, he was there from the beginning, helping to keep my spirits strong through the chaos. I never knew how much he cared about me until I acquired these conditions.

Though we have been labeled perfectionists, we know perfection is not real. On the contrary, our friendship is imperfectly perfect—just friends and no relationship drama. We inspire each other to keep achieving educationally, vocationally, and daily. Sometimes achievements are just enjoyment. We take pride in giving the most meaningful gifts, hugs, and songs. The simplest things, like our frequent text messages, playing intense Uno games, reciting silly rhymes in the hospital, him just rambling to me, or just meditating are much-needed rest stops on the marathon of achievement.

We both wish we could heal each other, but the reality is that we lead by our soles (souls) kept on toes, praying not to fall head over heels too far down, keeping afoot, heading forward on the journey with other feet along the way to keep our nerves from going off track, running. With all this, Brett always reminds me, "Remember, life's a marathon [AMARAthon], not a sprint, because one cell does not service every message [that] our whole selves need, so the new way of walking has healing ["heeling"] [capabilities] in itself."

If you read this, that is an achievement! Congrats! What do you aim to accomplish later or tomorrow?

Chapter 9
Dreams Coming True

A dream come true is a tucked away, mindful vision
that awakens your reality for all to see.

ALL MY LIFE, I HEARD the statements "Reach for the stars" and "Follow your dreams." Even Cinderella told me, "A dream is a wish your heart makes when you're fast asleep." I realized dreams are fantasies of the unconscious mind. When asleep, there is no control, but while awake, the fantasies have the possibility to come true. Truthfully, I hope the dreams I have when I sleep do not come true. Sometimes they match my daydream visions of greatness, though many times they do not.

I've had a couple powerful dreams of seeing my loved ones, and there is one personal dream I will never forget. This profound dream happened to me in my early twenties, when I met my younger self. To this day, I still feel like I really met myself.

She ran to me, her light golden-brown curls bouncing as she jumped, and smiled. I spoke to her, and we hugged so tightly. I woke up with my arms crossed. I told five-year-old Amara, "Keep dancing because, girl, that's going to save your life."

Before I started becoming sick in 2017, I kept having dreams I was in the hospital. Shortly after those dreams, I spent more than four months in hospitals that first year. Then six shorter inpatient hospital stays after that. Needless to say, some dreams are very realistic, and others have a very little chance of coming true.

I started to write this chapter as I watched the 2016 Olympics. These athletes overcame adversities, followed their passions, and became champions. Whether they won medals or not, just to make it to the Olympics is an accomplishment. Only a small percentage of training athletes make it. Despite the number of people achieving what seems to be a similar goal, dreams coming true are very individualistic. For a lot of us, some dreams are as simple as obtaining a job. A step further in that dream may be working at a job that we are passionate about. However big or small, dreams are those things in life that seem light-years away from fulfillment.

Each dance, music, or variety performance I have done, even just in front of a small audience, has been part of an essential aspect of my dream. Once one dream comes true, it just encourages me to believe in making the reality of another dream even brighter. By the age of twenty-two, I had several dreams come true. I am inspired by television shows such as *America's Got Talent*, and I even auditioned for it with my brother Rob in a variety comedy act. Being physically independent and able to attend and graduate college with a BA, and also attend graduate school, was a dream come true. Several years back, I thought that sounded too good to be true. Well, I was right, as months later, I acquired a life-changing illness. My body deteriorated at a rate I thought was slow, but it was actually coming on fast and causing a 75 percent loss of functional abilities in four months that has never stopped. Regardless of where I am now, I cannot take my former magical experiences away or dismiss the idea that there is still somehow something to gain from all this.

Right now, I am thinking back to a freshman orientation presentation by inspirational speaker and author Curtis Zimmerman, who spoke about living the dream. I was also inspired by his performance book I read. Basically, it was about how we are the lead characters in our own shows. My favorite point that Zimmerman makes is his suggestion that instead of saying "good" or "OK" when someone asks how you are, start saying, "I'm living the dream." Maybe at first, it'll be a lie, lying on a bed; yet slowly, it can await you to wake up to a dream-turned-reality.

I was living the dream then. Now, in a slightly convoluted way, I am still living the dream. My professional experiences helped in every aspect of my personal life as I learned to become my own therapist.

Creating my own nonprofit organization was a dream come true, as I have been able to share my gift and aid others in need of hope. The true dream is the journey of giving. This includes expanding outreach so we can help more individuals, families, and communities.

During my sophomore year of high school, I wrote an essay about what I dreamed of. I wrote about how I wished for cures of all serious chronic illnesses in the world and love for all. These dreams are things many of us wish for. In an ideal world, this would be possible. Sadly, this dream is as complex as the realm of dream ideology itself. However, humanity and nature are always unpredictable. My hero, Martin Luther King Jr., made his "I Have a Dream" speech more than fifty years ago. Did his dream come true? The answer is subjective, but dreams evolve with time and are usually too large to fit within a time frame. The reality is dreams of civil rights for all people will be an ongoing work in progress. As long as there is progress, that's what counts: keeping the dream alive.

Dynamic Dreams

Every child deserves to have even one small dream come true. Many have to wait until adulthood, but some do not make it and/or have much more difficulty getting there. That's why organizations like Make-A-Wish exist—to enhance the quality of life in children who are sick and give them an unforgettable experience.

In 2012, while researching to help my friend who has a severe brain injury, I discovered an organization called The Dream Factory of the Jersey Shore. This local chapter of the organization grants wishes to children and teens with chronic illnesses. These are many children who are not eligible for Make-A-Wish, yet they struggle greatly. I wanted to put in for a Dream Factory wish so that my dreams of helping others would potentially come true. I sought a wish, and the fabulous dream ladies granted my wish of having a shopping spree at an art shop in New York City, where I bought arts and crafts supplies for children to create, deliver, and use in my charitable programs. The store was near Central Park (one of my favorite places), where we visited and saw the Broadway musical *Wicked*.

The dream was so dynamic, allowing me to dance through life. It included a weekend of memories, but a lifetime of support and materials, which created countless smiles. My favorite and longest-kept items are the animal puppets, which brought so much joy in children's hospital puppet shows. This dream piloted my organization, career, and life mission. We have continued to share this resource with families we work with, allowing more dreams to be granted.

Magic of Dance: Best Night Ever

When I was young, I was afraid of the dark. As I grew older, however, I realized how special nighttime was. Throughout life, people like to have those nights of their dreams, whether it's high school prom or a special date. I had plenty of days to remember—and nights too—but not quite like the ones I dreamed of until the tenth anniversary of my accident.

I did not go to any homecoming dances, school proms, or college formals for a variety of reasons, mostly by choice. In the beginning of my acquired ataxia journey, I had no idea what was going on. However, I knew things were changing rapidly, and I dreamed of just having a special dance with all of my friends. More than a month later, at a banquet hall by the beach, I had a magic-themed dance to just celebrate life.

June 2, 2018 Journal Entry

June 1 is always an emotional day for me because it's the anniversary of my being hit by a car. It does hurt to think about everything, so this year I decided to have a colorful celebration of life and love to celebrate with my family, friends, and supporters. Events like last night mean so much to me. As my cousin Jessica said, "It was perfectly lively and intimate." I gained energy from all the positivity and magic. For those few hours, I forgot about the state I was in and all the worries of the future, and I just lived in the moment. I carried over my speech therapy mouth exercises naturally at the party! Even though things will get easier (like talking has for me), I know the most difficult parts are still to come. Knowing the support I have will make it so much easier! My mom rented a knee scooter for her foot and was having fun scooting around at the party as well. Now it's time for all of us to rest!

Thank you all so much for everything. I felt the most alive at the party than I have in more than six months. So here we go... I know I cannot just survive, but thrive. I'm praying I can thrive and dance more with independence, though no matter what this decade showed me, I can still D.A.N.C.E.

> *What you initially hoped for might just be the forgotten dream that leads you to the ultimate, ideal finish line. (Jessica Giannone)*

Amara having a blast at the Grenville Hotel for her anniversary celebration with friends Colin (Ch. 22) and Jess Kalamari (Ch. 17), 2018

Have you had one small or big dream come true? Keep dreaming.

Part 3
Nourish

The body is the water, the mind is the air that moves it, and the soul is the fire that ignites it all.

Nourish: To promote growth of; nurture; to furnish or sustain.[36]

It's what we need to be more than the seed
The nature's good; commonly misunderstood
The more we nourish, the more we can flourish
The body, mind, and soul working together in harmony is
     the ideal goal

Amara and Jessica being silly, April 2019

EVERYTHING WE CONSUME, FROM WHAT we breathe to what we eat and interact with, affects us either in negative ways or positive ways. This chapter isn't going to tell you what to eat or how to act in order to fuel your whole self. This chapter will merely remind you of your individual potential for fostering growth. Everyone feels nourished by different things. Yet we all have certain physiological and psychological entities to help us reach our greatest selves.

(Sometimes, it just comes down to appreciating the little things, like a good meal):

> That was the absolute greatest meal I ever had. You outdid yourself. It was healthy, balanced, fine dining. (Uncle Neil Giannone)

In 1943, humanistic psychologist Abraham Maslow developed a hierarchy of needs to demonstrate human motivations. It is a helpful theory (in the form of a pyramidal chart) in the fields of psychology and health, which signifies the levels of basic human necessities (from a psychological standpoint). The bottom of the pyramid starts with physiological needs, then continues to psychological needs, eventually getting to self-fulfillment and (rare) self-actualization. I agree that one must be nourished with the most basic needs to reach the top of the pyramid. However, I like circles more than pyramids. I don't think all basic needs have to be met in order for an individual to reach his or her higher self. A person can be living with serious health ailments or financial circumstances and still achieve more on an individual level than someone who is perfectly healthy and/or wealthy.

Nourishing all aspects of the hierarchy together can be challenging. For example, eating sweet treats may be great for the mind and spirit, but not so much for the body. Exercise, on the other hand, is great for the body, though some souls and minds just do not connect to the movement. Some people might focus entirely on holistic methods to heal themselves, where others, like myself, believe in the balance of both. I found a positive difference with using organic tube feedings compared to the processed ones given at hospitals. Some illnesses are cured just by nutrition. However, practices like cranio-sacral therapy,[37] reiki,[38] yoga, and meditation have also helped me throughout the years. Mindfulness is a practice I began using every day, thanks to the help of the *Calm* app. It's truly life-changing. Again, just as an individual can find fulfillment through different (not necessary all) needs, varying forms of nourishment can create their own harmony.

In my opinion, positive influences in the environment, in addition to participation in activities, are two of the most important forms of nourishment. On the extreme level, lack of nourishment can ultimately lead to major public health crises, such as substance abuse, obesity-related health problems, crime, and sexually transmitted diseases.

The physical activity of dance is my ideal form of whole-body nourishment; hence, it's the bridge to my philosophy. It allows us the freedom we deserve.

> Freedom is the whole body, spirit, and mind
> Given right to all, but each so one of a kind

Chapter 10
Body

We must hold our bodies with care, as they are our structural holding places for physical life.

Think about this:

> In one person there are more than 600 muscles and 200
>   bones
> Five vital organs…and it's 2018; still no clones
> Skin, hair, face, and shape are what we see with the eye
> Yet that picture is often a lie
> Made to identify, support, and protect
> Bodies are the surface of how we connect
> With each ma'am, sir, and circumstance we face
> They bring us from place to place
> Made to be strong and survive
> Giving our bodies love to help them thrive

MY GRANDMA WAS ALWAYS FASCINATED by how every single person on this earth, even an identical twin, has a unique face and body. The structures within them are different but have functional similarities. I always thought that was amazing too. Bodies fascinate me in all their aspects, especially women's. The process of babies being born can be mind-boggling. Our bodies are made for good—to help create, experience, and enjoy life. If just one process in each of our brains, blood, or organs goes out of whack, it affects the quality of life. However, there's usually something going right elsewhere in our bodies to compensate for the other complications. Nonetheless, taking care of our bodies, which allow us to truly move, live, and have adventures, is priceless.

I learned just how amazing our bodies truly are. Our brains are the control centers of everything. They're the reason we can wake up in the morning to breathe, swallow, talk, walk, think, and feel. Cells in our blood clot so we do not bleed out (that's what causes scabs). Temperature rising in a fever helps fight off infection. Tears cleanse the body. Passing gas releases toxins. Pain reminds us we have sensation. Coughing helps to clear out mucus. Hiccups regulate our digestion. When we are in danger, our brains warn us by physically triggering fright, and we react through a fight-or-flight response. Neuroplasticity in the brain allows it and the body to regenerate itself naturally after an injury. Typically, the body heals itself from a virus with no treatment. These are just some reminders of the importance of taking care of our bodies so that our bodies will take care of us in return.

As someone with an illness and acquired disability, it can be more difficult to love and appreciate a body that is not functioning properly. Currently, I am typing this as a physical body with a brain that is struggling to cooperate. It's August 2018, and my bent fingers touch the keys as I'm tilted back in my wheelchair with my head down and secretions filling my mouth. I try to remind myself that bodies are always changing due to environment, lifestyle, disease, and aging.

You know, as I grew up, I valued movement. Gymnastics and dance were my favorite activities, as well as playing sports with Rob. Training my body to be at its strongest made me feel strong on the inside too. After my accident, the goal was to keep moving as much as possible through rehabilitation. Although my progress is limited, exercise in any form nourishes my overall physical needs. I love dancing because I feel the same joy of moving, despite the fact that movement has changed tremendously. I had to adapt to my environment.

Everything around us affects our health. Society definitely influences how we nourish our bodies. Emphasis on work leaves less time to sleep, which is a crucial part of the human process in an overall healthy lifestyle. Then there are stronger negative influences—substances such as alcohol, cigarettes, and recreational drugs, which slowly decrease physical and brain function. In contrast, I know cannabis is a true lifesaver for many, and small amounts of wine can be beneficial in a number of ways. I never used any of these substances, yet my health still declined. I am not a doctor or health expert, so this is not meant as professional advice; just for the purposes of awareness and sharing my story: I believe that while emotionally we need self-love, physically we should try to do the same.

Look at You

All my life, I loved to take pictures and be on stage. I felt seemingly privileged for my dancer body, strutting around many times in revealing outfits. After my accident and illness, I became more conservative, but I was still proud of my disabled body.

Since late 2019, I preferred not to have pictures taken of myself because my appearance does not show what I believe to be the person I am. Without my smile, eyes open, or head up, who I am seems to remain hidden. However, I realized we're all struggling with our own self-images and body issues, and we should celebrate holistic beauty. Who I was before is still who I am now. My eyes are still green, though unseen, and my smile lies within my pathological grin.

For decades, societal focus has been on body image. There always seems to be a new diet or fitness fad. Now, there is an increased mainstream focus on taking care of the body for health reasons and not solely looks. I feel as though almost everyone goes through love-hate relationships with their bodies. Some men, such as my brother Rob, have struggled with confidence issues because they want to get big and strong. Rob eventually did gain a nice amount of muscle. What does too skinny, fit, or fat mean anyway? It's about loving yourself and giving your own body what it needs to allow you to be the best you can be—not to meet certain standards.

My mom and I, who are both on opposite sides of the body spectrum, strive to be fit despite changes in our bodies. Even the mass media is starting to emphasize that everyone's body is not made to fit in a particular figure. The idea of a body being perfect is a thing of the past, because, well, isn't everybody beautifully unique? Some are just more bodybuilding-conscious than others.

Hormones?

"It's just a hormonal imbalance." For much of my life, my mom and I have recited this phrase when things in our bodies became physically wacky. It is true that crazy things happen when there's an imbalance with internal fluids (which allow organs such as the brain, kidney, pancreas, liver, thyroid, ovaries, and testes to function properly). A factor in my acquired illness was my immune system attacking my thyroid and my brain, causing a downward spiral. Female hormones are even more complicated, which may explain why we are more prone to autoimmune disorders and certain mental illnesses. All the women I know, including myself, literally felt physically or mentally debilitated at least once because of an atypical menstrual cycle. Hormones acting up tend to intensify other illnesses, especially mental.

Though there is always a bright side. We also have happy hormones: endorphins. Endorphins are typically increased by exercising, sunlight/vitamin D, and organic food. Any time you feel yourself slipping, try to treat your body to an endorphin boost. Regardless of the ups and downs, I am thankful that my hormones allow me to experience my emotions fully and deeply. It helps to keep all this in mind when we feel our bodies going berserk.

More Body Talk

Do you know what listening to your body is like? For as long as I can remember, I have been told, "You're not listening to your body." I was always taught to just keep going. This isn't always ideal.

In a dance class when I was eleven years old, after three rotations of tumbling passes, I was apparently tired and undercut my back tuck. I went into a semiconscious state. I'm not sure if it was a concussion. I did not remember anything until I was sitting in a chair. My fellow students had to tell me what happened. They said I was crying and hitting my dance teacher, saying, "I'm fine." I did not go to the hospital, and my mom wasn't called until hours later. I continued to dance, flip, and go on with my day. I do remember the feeling of my head pounding, but the situation could have become way worse. Now that I'm aware of concussions and brain injuries, I am extra grateful I was all right. Nowadays, incidents like this are taken way more seriously.

Even after the above incident, I used to push on with my days, ignoring any alarming symptoms I experienced. When I started losing my voice in 2017, people even told me to stop talking and to relax. Maybe that would have helped, but my neurological condition was happening regardless. I listened to my body when I was tired and made sure to take naps every day, as well as take breaks and exercise. What I realized is that knowing when to take a breather is an extremely important part of nourishment. Now, I have no idea what my body is saying anymore, so it's hard to listen unless it makes a dramatic change, such as uncontrollable tremors (my signal to stop).

Taking care of yourself physically is about knowing patterns of your body and listening to it, even when your mind disagrees. Your body will talk, make noises, cause sensations, and make you struggle. Try to compromise with it like you would with a person. Make adaptations. If that doesn't work, you know who's boss. Regardless, it's your body, and your mind and soul have a say in how you choose to fuel it.

> I'm fine…just got my booze, cigarettes…going to lie in the sun. Everything in moderation. Life is good. (Uncle Neil Giannone)

How do you feel about your body? Is there something you can do to make yourself feel better about your health?

Chapter 11
Mind

*If the body can climb up a hill, the mind can help it
reach its peak to the mountains.*

MY MOM ALWAYS TOLD ME that if my mind was intact, I would be
fine. I agree; our thoughts, feelings, and behaviors impact the overall
quality of life. They contribute to our actions and our circumstances.
Mentality can either be a barrier or a carrier in this ideal life. Our
thoughts and emotions can cause actions that prevent us from reaching our full potentials, yet they can also empower us to reach heights
that are seemingly impossible.

FYI:

*Psychologists stress that our minds are actually more creative when
faced with hardships. It's in our nature to surpass obstacles. Your brain
likes to solve problems because it's designed to compensate for other setbacks. Under adversity, it forces itself to adapt. It's survival.*

I follow laws that align with my moral beliefs. The only field
of law I understand is the law of attraction. This universal love is
based on a principle that we create what we think and thus attract.
Visualization can nourish what we desire, as well as positivity.
Negativity, in turn, can draw negativity. This law often blames people for their circumstances. I believe, however, that there are other
reasons why things happen as well, some being no reason at all—
until one searches for it.

Decision-making is a complex process that is a huge factor in nourishment. Even common recreational circumstances can trigger a simple dilemma. Do you escape a troubled mind by getting wasted on alcohol, drugs, or cigarettes, or do you do something to help nourish your mind? It is difficult to sacrifice our immediate impulses and desires for more beneficial results sometimes. Maybe it takes time and some mistakes, but the most important thing is what you learned from them. Past decisions always influence the decisions we make in the present and in the future. Some choices, like what color shirt to wear, are not as huge as choices related to meaningful relationships, college, or other medical, professional, and financial choices. Give yourself for closure. Forgive. We learn, and we move on. Questioning yourself does not change what already happened. Letting go gives your mind and soul the freedom and peace it needs.

Choice that Has Given Me My Voice

Every choice my family and I have made has led me to who I am. I wonder how different my life would be if my family chose to move to that house in Old Bridge, New Jersey, instead of renting in another town and then moving to Howell. What if I chose to go to a different dance school? Would I have gotten hit by a car? Well, it doesn't matter because I truly feel as though God knows what I am meant for.

Some things happen beyond our control. My ataxia has given me a lack of coordination known as drunk disease. Ironically, I never had more than a sip of alcohol in my life because I knew with my brain injury that the consequences could be detrimental. I never did recreational drugs or participated in extremely risky behavior. I do feel at fault for jolting my injured brain by trying to flip on trampolines after the accident, doing my best to bend myself like I used to. I didn't feel as good doing it, but I let my child self take over.

Even though many things are beyond our control, we can still control how we handle the situations and hands we are dealt. It's important to feed the mind with necessary goodness so we can live life with the happiness we deserve despite other circumstances bringing us down. Therefore, taking care of the mind is important for overall well-being.

Our thinking is enhanced the more we use the thinking aspects of our brains while balancing the rest, of course. Some cognitive nourishment activities are writing, reading (I love audiobooks), doing puzzles, and engaging in various games that encourage critical thinking. The brain is the control muscle, and as they say, "Use it or lose it." Expressive activities and simply talking to a friend can release negativity and stimulate the brain. Positive thinking, affirmations, and partaking in activities that you enjoy help cleanse the mind. These activities certainly help me to be my greatest self, allowing me to stay in control mentally, even though my body is physically out of whack. Learning to adapt physically has correlated with my positive mental adaptations as well.

Continue to keep in mind that environments, experiences, genetics, and chemical makeup in the brain all help cultivate mindset. Nourishing surroundings and opportunities significantly increase a person's mental state. However, sometimes we are not in control of how we think, feel, and act. Extra care may be needed for the mind, just as if you need help for your body because of an illness. The amount of money, resources, and opportunities do not always make one less susceptible to mental health struggles. Remember, if one has malnourished his or her mind, it can be renourished. I cannot utter that loud and clear enough.

On this note, I think most people have personally known someone who has abused substances or have even abused substances themselves. Addictive disorders run in my extended family. While there is a substance abuse epidemic, I am honored to have been connected to the Regan family and their organization (CFC Loud N Clear) that is nourishing the needs of the community with recreation, education, and holistic health.

Out of His Shell

He was my first visitor during my 2017 hospital stay. At rehab, he made a turtle for me out of Play-Doh. One instance, as my nurse wheeled me down the block, he talked to me as he was shirtless fixing his car. We were laughing because I had a little stuffed turtle that made me jump when its arm snapped.

Marcus is like a second little brother, a neighbor and Rob's best friend (my favorite out of his homies). He is very kind, handsome, charming, and thoughtful—a skateboard-loving young man who decided to be the wise tortoise through an initiative to help himself reach his full potential.

At age twenty-two, he was partying every weekend and getting lit with his crew. Rob and his friends were able to stop and move on. Marcus, however, has addiction in his family, and he cannot just have one drink or just weed. Eventually, he told my brother how he was struggling and couldn't control himself. Unlike most his age, he told his parents what was going on and that he needed help. This is a true sign of strength. Within two weeks, he was off to an inpatient rehab facility where he stayed one month.

What's also inspiring is Marcus's courage. He always had difficulties learning in school, usually needing to take things slower, yet he still did his best to read my skits during the hospital volunteer visits, and he handwrote me the kindest letter when he was in rehab on his journey to sobriety. Marcus said, "I came out of my shell and sang karaoke SOBER." He told my brother he was scared at first, and being in the addiction program showed him he really was addicted, yet there was hope.

Now he is rebuilding his life, trying to live and love each moment in Queens, New York. When I hear his voice on the phone, my inner voice just screams, "I am so proud of you, li'l bro!" We all miss him and know once the coronavirus passes, slowly and steadily, our time will be turtle-y terrific.

Maniac

"She's a maniac, maniac on the floor...dancing like she's never danced before."[39] This was the song for my acrobatic jazz solo during my fourth-grade dance recital. It was my first year in New Jersey. I performed in ten numbers total. I was such a wild child on the stage;

the song title was fitting. All my extended family and friends came to that recital; I am truly blessed.

I wore my cousin Jessica's old dance costume: a hot-pink neon-colored ensemble with a '90s-type Velcro halter top. Since I was rushing between numbers, I must not have secured my top enough. I did not have any undergarments—just my bare, flat child chest. In the midst of my energetic dance moves and flips, my top came undone. Slowly it started falling down. It never even occurred to me to stop dancing, though I tried fixing it while I made up some steps on the spot.

Toward the end of the routine, I just stopped fixing it and did my side aerial into a split pose with my shirt down. I promise you that besides my "getting changed in nursing home beds" dances, erotic dancing is not my thing (though I totally respect burlesque).

After the performance, I had a meltdown of tears. All the dance students and teachers thought it was amazing that I just kept dancing. My mom did say people in the audience were saying rude things, appalled of the situation. But my family did not care. I heard them screaming my name over the music and hundreds of people. Maybe we need to treat life like a grand dance recital.

Have you ever had a major wardrobe malfunction on stage or an embarrassing malfunction in life? My Uncle Neil and my father's best friend, Greg, would think of this embarrassing moment of mine as my defining moment, as Uncle Neil put it.

"Absolutely awesome," Greg said. "That maniac dance was the moment I knew you were a superstar."

Uncle Neil would repeatedly remind me decades after the performance. He and Greg obviously greatly appreciated entertainment and adored how passionate I was. They both can relate to the song "Maniac" too, as they were happy drinkers. When they were on a high, it was an indescribable elation of mania we all fell into with them.

The summer after I graduated high school, both men were living at our house. Those were some crazy times, as our family was sometimes questioning, "Are they ever going to leave our home?"

Sadly, both are no longer with us. They each had a long downward spiral of mental illness. However, we will treasure these maniac memories forever. Thinking back now, although their welcome was not overstayed, I am grateful for their presence. Sometimes we have to channel our inner maniacs and just keep dancing because that's the best thing we can do in uncontrollable situations. Maybe if we act like maniacs without harming others, it's just extraordinary fun.

> Moments of shame
> May be part of our fame
> So much more than a name

Crazy

Crazy is a word thrown around like crazy: "My family is crazy; when I shook its tree, a bunch of nuts came out," "...is driving me crazy." I happen to like acting and being with people who are crazy because, to me, it could mean passion and excitement. So what's the actual definition? How can we positively support our cray-cray in life?

According to *Merriam-Webster, crazy* can mean "impractical, erratic, unusual; out of the ordinary; distracted with desire or excitement; absurdly fond; passionately preoccupied."[40]

(I would argue that many of these qualities can be endearing.)

I think the word *crazy*, like most adjectives, is based only on someone's perception of what is strange. If someone doesn't think he or she has acted crazy at one point in his or her lifetime, I think that is crazy, delusional. For example, having verbal conversations and arguments with yourself aloud is deemed crazy to some and normal to others. I do not like certain connotations of the word because it implies danger. Yes, someone with a mental illness, especially antisocial personality disorder or schizophrenia, can act very dangerously. (It is important to be careful because untreated people can commit horrific acts.) This does not mean all people who appear crazy have the intention to harm or murder you. It is very unlikely.

Just from living with my brother Lawrence, who has mental illnesses, I realized if someone like him can make another person feel crazy, imagine what it must feel like for Lawrence. Hearing my brother say the same words, play the same song, or move in the same way over and over like a broken record feels like we befriended insanity in those moments. It's more like an enemy that plays with my brother's and millions of other people's brains. That is not even in regard to the psychosis episodes. Imagine a hotpot of homemade sauce thrown across the kitchen with everything else and tantrum tornadoes. Lawrence's everyday crazy is not that extreme, but sometimes it does seem endless for us all.

I often think back to my crazy neighbor from Staten Island. It was like a sitcom, even though the moments when he invaded our space and displayed destructive behavior were too serious to laugh about. He was just a child, eight months older than me, doing his best in crazy circumstances with mental health. Now, many years later, I feel such joy from his comedic *Instagram* videos. He found his passion in comedy, art, and acting. Needless to say, this clown literally gave me nightmares, yet I am so grateful to have such fun times in childhood with a boy who is now a man: "Mr. Hollywood."

My buddy Scott, who was a client/helper at a camp I worked at, called me a crazzzy personality (in a funny and loving voice). Hey, without crazy, there would be no drama or entertainment, and without the crazy, catching those Zs might be more difficult. We must nourish the CRAZY, finding the parts of it that are **C**reative, **R**esilient, **A**uthentic, **Z**esty, and **Y**ours.

Do you talk about mental health and discuss taking care of your own mind? How do you cope with life's stressors? What can you do to be more mindful every day?

Chapter 12
Soul

Ridiculousness is necessary for the soul.
—Jessica Giannone

HAVE YOU EVER LAUGHED so hard that you had trouble breathing, got hurt, fell over, or became incontinent? Well, that is extreme…but in these instances, your soul was being nourished to the max.

One of my favorite ways to nourish my soul is through laughter. My Uncle Neil, for instance, made everyone laugh, even if we were angry with him (all the males in our family have a wacky sense of humor). Everything was just so comical with him. *Humor saves us in a way.*

He made monkey noises and faces when I woke up from my coma. I responded for the first time with somewhat of a smile. He inspired my passion for laughter and humor to use as a therapeutic tool.

The benefits of laughter and humor are no joke, as I read countless evidence-based practices and research articles about its benefits in various settings. Even though pretend laughter is a yoga exercise, it can also evoke positive feelings that bring authentic laughter. Physiological and psychological benefits include increased oxygen intake, lowered blood pressure, strengthened muscles, reduced pain, decreased stress hormones, promotion of social interaction, better attention, and higher self-awareness and quality of life.

(Despite the glorious benefits of some practices, it's always helpful to be aware of all outcomes. There is risk to everything, even laughter. Be sure to use humor carefully, as it is subjective. Since

107

laughing can also increase the heart rate, be wary of respiration that can cause other harmful symptoms in some patients if pushed too much.)

Although most laughter experiences were positive for me, due to my lack of muscle control, laughing has caused severe hiccup spasms, acid reflux, fatigue, and other annoying symptoms. In the hospital, my feeding tube would explode because I laughed with my friends so much. In another instance, a terminally ill teenage boy I worked with loved to laugh and have fun; it felt great that we made him happy, but I learned after to balance it out, as he always had increased symptoms pertaining to his lungs when we left. Can you literally die from laughter? Well, there have been reported cases over the years—the demise due to cardiac arrest or lack of oxygen supply to the body. But we can rest assured that the other positive qualities of the phenomenon are normally meant to balance it out.

Even when I'm sad, annoyed, or angry, my cats, brothers, or close friends can make me laugh at something. I tend to laugh at myself and my memories as well. I think it's important to have at least one person in your life whom you can laugh with without saying a word to. This is how I met and acquired many of my dear friendships. Television and movies can also bring that lighthearted laughter to detract the mind from stressors. Giggles can help take the focus off stressful circumstances by altering your perception of them, as you release multiple emotions as well. Sometimes all we can do is laugh!

My younger brother Rob was always the class clown and comedian of the family. As I grew more confident in myself, I became a comedian in my own right with my punny theatrics. I started doing stand-up, though I was still sitting down. I am thankful the ataxia did not take away my growing sense of humor, which brain injuries can do, depending on the affected area of the brain.

I used to implement humor/laughter therapy programs in my therapy work as well. My favorite places to participate in laughter programs were the nursing homes. The residents had opportunities to fully let go and enjoy the moments. I combined principles of drama, dance, and music using silly props to help enhance the process. All these activities are meant to stimulate joy. Smiles and laughter are so contagious. When one person laughs, it spreads to others.

The majority of my happiness, especially in my teen/young adult years, came from reaching out in the community by giving pick-me-ups through my organization. My FAV (Friendly Ability Volunteer) program was a FAVorite of mine because I met like-minded youth and adults who wanted to make a difference. We each had our own quirks, but we came together to spread joy. I met the most amazing people and expanded my knowledge, all while sharing my gifts of writing, comedy, expressive arts, and inspiration to the world. Seeing the faces of joy and hearing testimonials such as "No need for morphine," "I now know what I need in life to recover," "First smile in weeks," "I realized it's OK to talk about my mental illness," and "You helped heal my son with the donation for treatment from the funds raised" is what makes me feel whole. My nonprofit continues to change, as do I, and I know this is what I'm meant to do, no matter how small or large.

To me, nourishing the souls of others in our communities is the most important thing to feed our souls. It is the best way to find your personal "soul" purpose, which is not solely done in one way. All my life, I knew I wanted to do more. I'm technically doing less right now (only writing this book), but it will hopefully allow me to give back even more in future in the grandest way.

PATHologically Amazing

In the maze of life, we cross others' paths that alter our lives forever. That's why it's a-mazing! In July of 2017, I decided to create a positive memory at a public park after I had a major panic attack days before. My amazing friend from graduate school (see chapter 17), whom I met earlier that week, played the guitar and sang while I danced, sang, and interacted with people in the community. One lady walking through the park thoroughly enjoyed our music, so I slowly invited her to sing and dance with us. I could visibly see she had some type of disability, as she looked, talked, and walked a little differently. Through the music, this woman opened up to me about her story of living with HIV, having no family, having a developmental disability, surviving homelessness, and being abused. I invited her to have dinner with us later in the day, and she was ecstatic.

We met her at the park and walked to Harvard Square to get Chinese food. The forty-eight-year-old self-proclaimed survivor repeatedly told us about how thankful she was to meet us. She expressed, "God puts people in your life at the right time. I was starting to think negatively of the world because [of] all I [have] been through…then you come into my life, showing me that there are caring, nonjudgmental people in the world. Even more than the food, I loved just interacting with you."

This made my heart cry of happiness because I believe this is what I am here on this earth to do. I invited her to my dorm a week later as well. We had no way of communication between visits, just word of mouth and trust. It felt so good to help her and her friends at Harvard Square.

A funny, soul-expressing moment from this deed was when we were all in the process of letting go of anger, screaming and dancing in the park. A young man from Ireland was videoing us, probably as a joke. Some people do not understand soul work; they seem to be doing what I like to call oversitting (the opposite!). Regardless, with passionate, creative people bringing arts to clinical settings and communities, the world will become more just, accepting, and caring. Turning around my park experience from a negative to a positive is congruent with my life's mission, and it opens my eyes to the life around me.

Lots

"I'm sorry I am a lot," I said, after struggling to find a position to type.

"Were you ever a little? You are worth it, girl," my community skills therapist, Casey, told me.

She always has a way about her that nourishes my soul, positively affirming my attributes and helping me to adapt to live my best life. Casey was my therapist for a year and a half, and now she is my friend (who also befriended Jessica after five hours on the phone). Casey and I have a lot of values, interests, and ideology in common. She is one of the most compassionate, pure, genuine, environmentally friendly, mindful, and nourished women I ever met.

Casey has watched me go through a lot of difficult declines, always bringing me back to the moment. Casey often reminds me of the poem that states, "People are in our lives for a reason, season and/or lifetime." I think my Jersey Shore, cat-loving friend is all three.

Do you like to laugh? Are there people in your life who fill up your soul with pure joy? What can you do to lift your spirit and the spirits of others?

Chapter 13
Leisure and Recreation

My work is my play, and play is my work, so it never feels like work anyway.

LEISURE CAN REFER TO ANY or all of the following: unobligated time, an unhurried or enjoyable state of being, and simply freedom from demands. One widely accepted element of leisure is that it is not work.[41]

Recreation describes actual participation in an activity, usually in a more structured manner and involving more socialization. Both are needed to help humans develop and enhance well-being.[42]

As a recreational therapist who believes she has a fun job, the above quote can feel true. Of course, there is still a difference between personal recreation/leisure and implementing recreational opportunities for others. I actually feel the essence of flow (complete happy focus) when I am doing what I love. I believe recreation and leisure truly are the nourishment we all need for the body, mind, and soul. Time off from occupational life helps one's overall health, happiness, and balance. Daily leisure activities such as watching television, chatting with friends via technology, checking social media, reading, and working out can help us unwind from our days. Recreation should be inclusive to people of all backgrounds and abilities. It's a goal society is working on. This is why I became a certified therapeutic recreation specialist.

Developmentally, children reach milestones through socialization, playing, and interacting with the environment. Older adults greatly benefit from recreation and leisure to keep active, stimulated, and enhance the quality of life. Some of the greatest memories come from leisure and recreational experiences—great adventures, accomplishments, friendships, and self-growth that can transfer onto everyday tasks.

Different cultures and families view leisure and recreation differently. I'm thankful my family valued the importance of being involved in activities and social functions. From early on, my brothers, cousin Jessica, and I experienced the greatness the world had to offer from going on family vacations, playing with toys, and participating in many recreational activities. Dance became my most focused activity later on in childhood. Additionally, I also participated in swimming, karate, soccer, basketball, choir, and the school drama club. In my free time, I had a lot of playdates, and I often played with dolls, board games, jumped on the trampoline, went to the park, read, wrote, and made art. I still do many of the same things, just obviously differently to fit my age and current physical ability level. Intrinsic motivation—doing something for internal joy and not external rewards—is vital for overall well-being.

Rob's Rec-Creations

Once upon a time, I was a puny little boy without an ounce of muscle on me.

Growing up as a child, I always became bored very easily because I had high energy for physical activity and a short attention span. However, I would never lose focus playing or watching sports, as I always loved the competitive nature of it. I was typically the smallest in my classes or organized teams. I never made excuses about my size; not to mention the first word that ever came out of my mouth was "ball." Sports undoubtedly had such a big impact on my life from the start. I did not care if I was dribbling, catching, kicking, or throwing a ball. I was always entertained as long as I had a ball in my hands.

I stood under five feet until I was 14 years old, so I was an underdog...who not many people expected to be a contributor during athletic competitions. I was also never the most skilled or the most athletic at soccer, basketball, wrestling, or football. Although, one thing I had was heart, as I made sure that I would give it my all to ensure victories for my teams. I hate to say it, though, I was a sore loser, and I could not stand losing.

There was one instance when I was 11 years old and scored 20 points—the most I ever scored in a game. While I should've been proud of my performance, I cried my eyes out as my team lost in a highly competitive basketball game. As a 23-year-old now, I completely understand that winning is not everything, but having a competitive mindset has helped me currently reach my fitness goals. I have turned my focus to improving my body.

Thankfully, I am much more confident with my figure, as sports taught me how to condition and weight-train my body. All in all, I learned that playing a sport is more than just an activity. It helped improve my overall mindset on life. Times can be tough, but even leisure, exercise, or a fun sport is a fantastic stress reliever; a teacher of life and a perfect community builder.

***

I am most inspired by my brother's home boys, a.k.a. neighborhood friends Andrew, Marcus, and Kyle. They truly live for the moment and always stick together through everything. Basically, my house is open for them at all times. Sometimes they do not make the wisest of choices, as they have broken many bones by performing skating tricks. They always want to hang out and have fun. People can judge them as being reckless, ruthless, irresponsible young adults. I look at it from the perspective that they are making and learning from mistakes. My brothers and friends value leisure time the same way I do. We just have different definitions of fun.

From personal and professional experience, I learned that recreation is extremely beneficial for people who have disabilities. I never recognized its value until I truly needed it in my life, as I have been in and out of hospitals and rehabilitation centers. Emotionally and physically, recreation helps in my recovery, keeping me strong. Community outings have always been important to me because they helped me feel more comfortable leaving the hospital and going home.

For my family, going out in the community consists of much more planning and assessing of the accessibility and time factors. Because of Lawrence's autism, we try to avoid huge crowds, and we go places where we can be in a corner. At the same time, not all places adhere to the Americans with Disabilities Act due to various reasons, so we try to investigate beforehand. The takeaway from this is that recreation is recreated uniquely by each individual participant.

Not every party is enjoyable, of course, partly because of attendees and the atmosphere. There are times when it's just a party of one—just me. Those parties can be lonely and upsetting, but they also can be the best occasions for self-discovery, relaxation, and achievement. Learning to enjoy time with a party of one is not easy, but it can definitely be done! In any case, I am thankful I have a fun family to share my time with.

My family just loves to play games. Our game nights provide the greatest memories, and playing games really brings people together while stimulating the brain and the body. From innocent Scrabble and charades to chess and poker, games can also get intense. We must remember that at some moments, even leisurely activities can have detrimental consequences. (Severe competitions can destroy relationships, cause a loss of financial stability, and even rip apart lives).

When having fun takes fundamentals away from a person, that's not funny anymore! Play away, but play responsibly.

In this party of life, we all need to be invited and dance together. Sometimes people simply need to let go of daily life and just enjoy. Some parts of the "part-y" go missing, and some are found through a party itself! There's a famous saying I can relate to: "Life may not be the party we hoped for…but while we're here we may as well dance." I am proud to say I'm the person who will dance alone on the dance floor. People may see me and think I'm a party girl. Truthfully, I've never been to a college party; I just used to love hosting parties for others and going to my loved ones' parties. (Similarly, my brother Rob is Mr. Party and also a DJ/emcee.) Bringing people together to dance and celebrate is one of my favorite parts of life. Nourishing a part of yourself with people who are usually apart from you is particularly soothing and, many times, the exact kind of entertainment you need.

Riding the Waves

At the beach
Surf's up, tide's low
Riding with eight
People who carried me
Flat on board
Let's go…

I crazy laugh each time
Waves crashed
At end
I went under
Got soaked
Couldn't see
Spit flowing
But I lived up
To my new surfer name
Showing you…Trixie

Tricks that were
Led by Operation Beachhead

Recreation…inspiration…motivation…

Other than the arts, I absolutely love swimming and being around water. This was my first time on the beach since my new illness and my first time ever surfing. I never thought about surfing because of previous balance issues, let alone new issues with my floppy self. The organization Operation Beachhead, started by veteran Michael Ricci, gives individuals of all ages and abilities the opportunity to experience water sports and other seasonal adventure/adaptive activities.

Most medical professionals and people are afraid to have me participate in activities like that, claiming I can't or shouldn't. Taking risks and overcoming pain, however, are worth experiencing in life, especially being in the sanctuary of water. As long as there are enough people and support in place, why not? I commend all recreation organizations, especially those geared toward people who have less opportunities (whether because of illnesses, disabilities, or financial difficulties). These charities are able to fulfill missions because of volunteers, and the passion and enjoyment is shared by all. With a little research, I'm sure there are resources located near you. If the something you are looking for doesn't exist, maybe you can begin something wonderful.

> Surfing those waves
> Love saves
> Water can get rough
> But we hang tough
> —"Riding the Waves," August 29, 2018

Monkey in the Middle (September 7, 2018)

Due to my condition, recently I've felt like I am youthing instead of my typical adulting. Well, maybe I'm just kidding. I feel like the monkey trying to hang onto the branches of life in the middle of a fallen forest. My brother Rob, his girlfriend Emily, and I went to a local park (the beautiful Manasquan Reservoir). After they had a little picnic, we decided to play a game. I forgot my bouncy ball, so all I had was a little stuffed sloth/monkey-looking thing. I remembered when I was a child playing monkey in the middle, so we all played in the playground. We were laughing, I had *Spotify* playing, and all of us were getting exercise. Imagine able-bodied twenty-, twenty-one-, and twenty-three-year-olds—one in a tilted wheelchair—all laughing and having a blast playing this childish game.

There were some young children around the ages of two to six playing on the slides and swings. Then I noticed two young teenagers sitting on a bench with extreme boredom painted all over their body language. I was impressed they had no phones on them and were so respectful to their mother. I can stereotype and say they were adopted based on racial differences, but I'm not sure. I asked them to come play with us. The brother and sister jumped up happily, very willing to join the game. We talked, laughed, and played monkey in the middle for about twenty minutes more until we left. The siblings' younger sisters started playing with us too. It was a magical start of September, highlighting the power of recreation and inclusion. All that was needed was a stuffed monkey and company (though my phone helped with the music). I guess this story shows that even in 2018, when technology reigns, the true royalty is in the form of the simple, old-fashioned leisurely pastimes of youth.

What do you enjoy doing for fun? How can you incorporate more leisure and recreation into your life?

Chapter 14
Inner Voice

*Playing with words is a never-ending game that I
love because I make up the majority of the rules, and
I always win.*

It screams but is unheard
Struggling to find the word
We all have a voice
To release it is our choice

WRITING MAKES THINGS RIGHT WHEN the world is going left. It gives
people a voice, which either emotionally or physically might not be
heard otherwise. We all have freedom of speech, and written language preserves that freedom. When I began to lose my voice due
my illness, writing became (and now is) more essential for me. It is
the voice that my anatomy struggles to convey. My words are written
here because of words, sentences, passages, and stories written before
me. Writing allows us to reflect, then later recollect.

Journaling, specifically, is an evidenced-based technique that
has helped people throughout their everyday lives and personal struggles. I find that journaling helps me clear my mind in a way that is
unfiltered and raw. Similarly, many people love social media because
they can share their voices and writing on a greater level. As a hom-
age to when I was younger and loved writing in journals, my parents
created a *CaringBridge* page for me after my accident. *CaringBridge*
is a charitable social media site that allows people facing medical conditions to have a supportive outlet to share their stories. It's a great

platform for people to stay updated on my progress and for me to express myself. It gives me a voice when I feel unheard.

Last, but certainly not least, in a world where words equal power, how can one be seen and heard as powerful? I believe this is through poetry. Poetry calls on the imagination to create images without visually displaying them. Creating a performance through speaking (the written art of rap or spoken word) is one of my favorite ways to honor and nourish the world. I love that poetry has rhythm, yet it does not have to rhyme. It's a fabulous formation that does not need form. It's an exaggeration of life, but it can speak true to reality.

As you know, I love all the arts, but writing is the hidden puppeteer that plays the puppets of my other artistic expressions. Poetry, to me, is music, visual art, dance, and drama written out on paper. It clarifies all my discombobulated thoughts and feelings into art. I enjoy writing poetry before or after I paint a picture or dance because it helps enhance my overall artistic process. Poetry is a tool I have also used with numerous patients I have worked with. In high school, I enjoyed performing professional poetry in Poetry Out Loud contests. In undergraduate school, I was defined by some as the poetry girl because I enjoyed expressing myself and listening to the written art of my peers at spoken word events, which inspired me to dive deeper into this art.

At a young age, I also loved writing Dr. Seuss-type poems—silly, happy, and carefree. As I experienced life, I learned that the most enlightening poetry often comes from a person in the darkest of places. I did not write the word *beautiful* because beauty can be deformed and puzzling (yet it's always effective). It's BE-YOUtiful, because it affects you. Some people may be afraid of not knowing how to write a poem, but some simple guidelines can help evoke the expression process. In class, I learned to free write (continuously writing without pausing to edit or think about it) before writing actual poems. Following a format can also be easier in instances such as writing haikus, couplets, or acrostics. My friend wrote a line using my words, and it resonates with me 100 percent: "I don't put my feelings on a shelf because I'm a fool of self."

(Haikus are Japanese-inspired poems that are usually about nature. They do not need to rhyme, and they have 5-7-5 syllable counts).

Rose
It stems from a thorn
Rises with love and beauty
The great Rose is born

Apple Tree
Fruit embarks sweet growth
Some fall down. Are they rotten?
No, it just needs some heat

Water
Pure liquid from earth
Essential changing form
Priceless is its worth

Acrostic poems are one of my favorite types because they are simple and can be written about any word. My D.A.N.C.E. acronym is my motto, but I wrote a few other mottos to match others' favorite hobby verbs to inspire them as well. Try to create your own!

B.A.K.E.
Believe your dreams are true
Achieve by being the best you
Keep kindness always
Enjoy the most out of your days

C.H.E.E.R.
Conquer your fears
Honor your peers
Enjoy simplicity
Energize like electricity
Radiate genuine love

S.I.N.G.
Shine your inner light
Inspire others to fight
Nourish self as whole
Give from your soul

Free-form metaphorical: A poem using a direct comparison, not pertaining to a particular rhythmic style, and usually abstract. My favorite example of this is Emily Dickinson's "'Hope' is the thing with feathers." I wrote a poem inspired by this about something that can prevent you from keeping that hope: fear.

Fear Is…

Fear is…the metal bars that keep us inside
A cage; trapped
Seemingly no room to move
Not like it even tried

It was broke and bent in the past
So now it needs to stay firm
Firmly screaming "NO"
Its voice doesn't last

Long, letting go…the structure fades
The wings of the soul take control
Did you know fear is afraid?
Of the silent power: YOU…for there is always HOPE!

Social Media

Many people like to share their voices via social media outlets such as *Facebook* and *Instagram*. Some post short, obscure captions, and others share every detail. Personally, I share exactly how I am feeling, typically in metaphorical terms. Here is an example of a couple *Instagram* posts in Amara style, minus the pictures (I love using pun play on words in most of my writings).

> Hats off to the weeks past
> Drop of a hat…life can change so fast
> The many different hats we wear
> Embody the roles we play and share
> Passing the hat around
> Pulling out of the hat the magic within we have found
> With ups and downs, this and that
> I'm grateful to create my own hat!

The above was part of a poem I used for a nursing home project in the spring of 2017, and I made a hat as well. I've been so thankful for each opportunity, being a part of a loving community and being able to help create unity in various settings. Thanks to my family, friends, FAVs, professors, and coworkers for helping me create each hat in separate situations but still allowing me to keep my original elements: flowers, colors, laughter, etc. Wishing everyone a wonderful week! Hats off to you! And together, we can do the hat D.A.N.C.E. Much love and prayers to all.

Rolling with Hawaiian PUNches (October 30, 2018)

Huh? Why? And…there's the
PUNch…helping us through the ugh…low…ha…
Yes, hello! Aloha! In this life, we keep it juicy, out of the
    box, rolling with the
Hawaiian PUNches

Happy almost Halloween, everyone! I knew I had to keep it juicy this year. So, yeah, it can get scary, but we keep fighting! Credits to my cool aide, Kool-Aid (Sophia), for helping me create this.

***

Language is so powerful that it literally can alter a mindset. Having positive, heartfelt, thought-out messages can be what someone needs to get through his or her day. So I advise you to write, whether with a pencil or a keypad. Write a letter, a poem, or even a cute text to someone who you might not always talk to. Write because it's your right to express your mess. Hold it close, or give it as a message to keep holding on.

Are there words in your head you just cannot process? Try writing them down in a journal, write a letter to someone, or maybe create a poem.

Part 4
Create

Nothing is the exact same; not one bit
    What you brought to the world is legit
    Oh, to take something is great; to make it is greater
    Better to begin now rather than later

The Riccios, 2012

HAVE YOU EVER WANTED SOMETHING so badly but could not seem to find it anywhere? The supposed object or information, of course, is not found in a store, *Amazon, YouTube,* or *Pinterest.* That means YOU have the power to bring it to life, whether in the form of artistic mediums, food, objects, or opportunities. This section of the book is my favorite because, in my life, it has influenced all other aspects of D.A.N.C.E.

Even while dancing physically, I was never fond of just learning steps, but of using my movements to create things that matched my emotions or told a story. Some of my most memorable experiences are related to creating and then sharing the creations with others. G. K. Chesterson, an exemplary English writer from the twentieth century, explains that "creation differs from construction in that creation is loved before it exists." Creation can be structured or spontaneous, and passion can be found in both creation and construction. The love is shown through a willingness to make a change and to express the self, values, and beliefs. Some say creating is like falling in love because you feel the same strong passion during the process without knowing where it's going to lead you.

When anything breaks in the house, my dad—a nontraditional handyman—always has a solution. His ideas are unconventional and sometimes silly (taping windows with duct tape, for example). My dad also says I get my creative dance moves from him, as he always showcases what he refers to as the Fusco shuffle, a dance he made up where he kicks his legs rapidly in a comedic manner. I learned that the greater my disability became, the more creative I seemed to become because I needed to find a way to work it out.

I live life in a creative wonderland. It's what helps me feel happy and function to the best of my ability. Creativity is a form of discovery that enables accomplishments, nourishes the whole self, and allows you to embrace the moment. Whether it's delving into an artistic form or playing and using innovation to solve problems, the sea ("C") of creativity is what makes the waves of life, preventing us from being tide (tied) down in stagnant water.

Chapter 15
Something New

NEW is something you never knew before
The freshest creations are fascinations…
Filled with spectualizations
How did it arrive?
How can we keep it alive?

THE NEWEST BABY, FRIEND, FASHION trend, TV show, song, or technological device often makes people go wild. (I personally feel a burst of internal energy when I meet, find, or make something new). All these new things eventually become old and forgotten until someone brings them back again with a new twist—a change. Changes, however, can be scary, especially when we do not have full control over them. Think of circumstances such as getting a new president or suffering a personal life tragedy. Despite setbacks like this, we have to remember that change is a natural part of life. Butterflies (a natural and beautiful phenomenon), for instance, show me that change is okay. We can hop into something—scared in a cocoon, falling down the rabbit hole until we fly away with a "new" that we created. Our creations change the world.

So how was the earth made? I was always told that God made the universe. How was God made? I never received an explanation after that. "Mom, someone at school told me we are all monkeys." These are all things I wondered about, like many of us do—great minds and all. Stephen Hawking, a remarkable physicist (and also an atheist), described the importance of ever-expanding knowledge and creation in human evolution. While he had a scientific explanation for our origins, others religiously attribute the mystery to an intelligent source. We may never know. However, this doesn't make our creations any less significant.

I believe all philosophical views have truths to them, and I definitely believe in a higher power of creation. Nevertheless, regardless of how humans made it here, we still create the future. Some creations are simply meant for pure enjoyment (which can absolutely be purposeful). I realized most inventions are made for the greater good of society: languages, methods of transportation, technology, houses, roads, appliances, etc. They're creations that help increase our entertainment, communication, health, and quality of life. Creations are more than objects; they're ideas and opportunities. Nowadays, it can be more difficult to create something new when so much has already been made. Though when someone experiences anger, frustration, or a conflict, that's when the courage to create comes roaring in like a lion!

Speaking of lion (lying), I believe dishonest people happen to be quite creative people who use their talents for injustice. Due to my mother's and my own trusting disposition, we have met people who lied about their entire lives to just be our friends. I know other people who were also blindsided by pathological liars. These liars are typically unhappy with situations in their lives, so they create stories to help benefit themselves, knowing this will eventually hurt them. It's a serious problem. My mother tells me that once someone starts lying, he or she eventually forgets the truth and cannot distinguish the truth from the lie. I know, for example, my brother excels at telling little white lies to avoid trouble, like many people. Exaggerations (and courtesy lies) do have their benefits on occasion, of course. However, those take less thought than flat-out lies, such as making up your family life, a serious medical condition, or personal history.

I experienced such an instance of extreme lying with a girl I met in college who was a grade younger than me and was also lonely and insecure due to her weight problem. I would talk to her and help guide her through all the struggles that she opened up to me about— struggles of battling cancer, having a father in jail, and three younger siblings who had severe disabilities, just to name a few. After meeting her parents, it all came out, and I was done with her. It seemed unreal that everything I knew was unreal. I cannot associate myself with dishonest people because every part of me is genuine. This is why I am sometimes weary of close relationships.

I'm sure you or someone you know experienced creativity gone wrong—harmful schemes and lies. Well, you could use all that information and write a fictional story. This book was meant to highlight the positive. So hang on; there's so much good that comes out of everyday creative practices, which you may have overlooked.

Hang Tight…I Have an Idea

I have always been innovative with artistic practices, but in other aspects, my critical thinking can be lacking. One of the many things I learned from my patients during my internship was to solve problems by reversing my normal way of thinking. One cold February afternoon, my patient (I will call her Dory) and I came back from a community outing. (Dory was in her forties and lived with multiple brain injuries, which did not impact her cognition. One of the difficulties was using her arms). With moderate assistance from me to take her coat off, she then wanted to hang it. The coat kept falling off the hanger. I kept trying to put it back on, slightly altering its position. I told her, "I'm sorry, I don't know why I am having trouble. Where should we put this?" Dory laughed and said, "Girl, you give up too easily." That tore me inside because I'm normally known as the creative person who does not give up.

Regardless, she told me to zip it and put it on the hanger. Sure enough, that was the solution I almost did not make happen. I thanked Dory, and from then on, I have been more aware of the idea of not hanging on to the same ideas. I zip my way to finding solutions. There's always something more to Discover, Accomplish, and Nourish so we can Create a new way to Embrace life to its fullest.

PeaceLove

Around 2009, a man from Rhode Island named Jeff decided to create peace of mind for himself by painting in order to aid in his struggles with obsessive-compulsive disorder. Soon, this personal movement expanded nationwide through an organization called PeaceLove. I feel honored to say I was awarded a scholarship to become a part of that movement and receive training to become a PeaceLove CREATOR. A CREATOR's mission is to deliver uniquely designed expressive arts workshops in his or her community. My training event took place in Pawtucket, Road Island, with other recreation therapists, counselors, educators, and social service professionals who wanted to learn new and creative ways to benefit clientele.

In February of 2017, I became certified after running thirteen workshops using visual arts, storytelling, sound, and movement with the purpose of providing new resources and skills that promote mental wellness. I continued running dozens more of these programs through Riccio Pick-Me-Ups for nursing home residents, volunteers, classmates, teens, and adults with brain injuries in local youth shelters. All projects emphasize the creative, therapeutic process and are geared toward starting conversations about mental health. The symbolism, multimedia, and community bonding aspects of the projects make them unique, enjoyable, and go-to tools in my practices. PeaceLove has never forgotten me as a CREATOR, which gives me greater peace of mind.

Amara intently focused on her "story shoe" in a
PeaceLove workshop in Rhode Island, 2016

*Have you created something new to better life for yourself
and/or others? How can you further create to fulfill your dreams?*

Chapter 16
Art

I think of art like the arteries that pump blood to the heart, fueling love; essential for the self and others.

EVERYTHING IN LIFE IS ART to me because it's created by someone else—in order to be further used to create something different thereafter. Like beauty, art is perceptual and radiates from the inside out. I think of it as using bodily and worldly sensations to help create a sense of purpose. Some art is intentionally made a particular way, and other art just happens unexpectedly. I have always loved all things artsy, but I never considered myself an artist due to lack of technical precision in my work. I guess I'm more abstract in every modality. Of course, art does imitate life after all.

My best friend from high school, Ilana, whom I believe is extremely talented in multiple art forms, told me I am a true artist because I live life as an artist. This is why I felt so honored and encouraged to follow my dream of using my professional experiences to become an expressive arts therapist. Learning and experiencing the arts in a therapeutic aspect increased my understanding and appreciation of it. You may be reading this thinking "I never liked art" or "I'm not creative." Let yourself explore; it may surprise you.

Some people are more suited to kinesthetic art, such as dance, while others may be more suited to visual art, such as painting or sculpting, but all art forms are connected so closely. That is why an artist usually has multiple passions and talents. In the following paragraphs, I'll briefly explain each modality (aside from poetry—see chapter 14) and how it has impacted my life, in addition to how it can help you as well.

Dance

As you know, out of all the art forms, this is the one I'm most comfortable with, even with my physical disability. I have felt from a young age the feeling of my soul moving when my body dances. I think I was a great dancer, despite my toes not being pointed correctly, arms not properly placed, or knees not entirely straight. I studied the classics, ballet, tap, contemporary, jazz, and my favorites: musical theater, hip-hop, and acrobatics. I competed at a few different schools since I was nine years old, but that was not my favorite part of dance. Although I enjoyed learning routines, I loved simply using improvisation dance everywhere (at my house, a store, school, a party, and wherever else I was). I am still like that with or without music. Let's just keep moving!

My best movement has been through facial expressions and bodily rhythm, like the soul moving through the body. After my initial accident, I was depressed because I wanted to dance like I did prior to my brain injury. A couple of weeks after my accident and a few days after waking from the coma, I went to a dance therapy workshop at the inpatient rehabilitation hospital I was in. I wanted to get up, kick, and leap. I didn't understand why my face had difficulty or why my body couldn't move like it did previously. I had to become educated on how to move in my wheelchair. After this, I knew I wanted to use dance as therapy.

Through years of recovery, I kept dancing and maximizing whatever abilities I had at the time until I gained enough skills to become a hip-hop dance teacher. I admire the extreme work ethic and passion that professional dancers possess. Though I loved dance more than anything, I knew even as a middle schooler that a professional dance career was not meant for me. My initial plan after undergraduate school was to become a dance/movement therapist. After some soul-searching, I learned that every art form uses movement, so I chose expressive arts therapy.

There are many barriers people face when moving their bodies freely in dance, such as self-consciousness and anxiety. Contrarily, once a person is given the space to move, without even realizing it, he or she releases stress that had been physically bottled up. I wrote a research paper in my undergraduate studies regarding movement therapy, and I have been to a couple of dance therapy workshops where I met a movement therapy pioneer, Fran Levy. Fran describes a technique called mirroring as "reflecting a deep emotional acceptance and communication." I move in a very unique way, making it difficult to copy exact movements. This is acceptable, however, because a mirror is not an exact representation of an image, but an echo.

We all have unique ways of movement in our daily lives that can be explored in a dance therapy technique called authentic movement. This is just an extension of how we move in our everyday lives. The practice involves free association of bodily movements and expressive improvisation of motion. Do we do things slow or fast? Are we stiff or loose? Is the breath light or heavy? Is it loud or soft? Is everything voluntary? I became more aware. I think being mindful of your movements and expressions can help you feel more confident in yourself, knowing you can achieve a uniquely creative presence. In my current situation with a movement disorder, authentic movement is all I focus on. I love this free form of dancing because my moves do not have to be functional, or even purposeful, to be expressive.

During my sophomore year of college, I wrote a fifteen-page research paper about the universal aspects of dance and how it increases confidence in people of all backgrounds, ages, and abilities. There were some contraindications,[43] depending on the style of dance and gender. Even in this age, many boys still feel ashamed of doing classical dance, such as ballet. Social dance, in my small study, had the highest correlation with increased self-esteem and confidence. Maybe it's because people feel better if they're not alone.

From the beginning of time—across all cultures—dance has brought people together. Movement paired with music and storytelling has helped millions heal from emotional and physical wounds. From the "Charleston," "Running Man," "Electric Slide," and

"Cotton-Eyed Joe" to the "Soulja Boy," "Cupid Shuffle," "Wobble," "Floss," and fads like Drake's "In My Feelings," many people enjoy having a format, though less emotion is involved. These are enjoyable and do bring people together, yet for me, the structure takes away creativity and freedom of movement. Everyone is different. We're learning on this journey together.

I only taught hip-hop dance classes for two months, but it was an indescribable, amazing experience each time. I felt the energy and excitement in every class. I choreographed and taught the students many dance steps, but I always made sure to emphasize freestyle. The process was a challenge. Half of them looked forward to expressing themselves with their bodies and having no rules. The other half were afraid, needing some encouragement and prompts by me. In any case, they all learned something new about themselves.

Before my later setback, I saw a psychic out of curiosity, and she said I was going to teach people dance as my life career. I was confused. I wanted to be a therapist. Why did she say this? Then I thought that maybe my D.A.N.C.E. motto would become more known. I was a therapist who used dance as one of my main tools. Now my original path is unexpectedly on hold, and dance is still my number one love. I wrote this book. It all comes back to the dance, which would not exist without the drama.

Drama

"Stop being so dramatic!" is a phrase my family has been telling me my entire life. Though I thought dance was a modality that came most naturally to me, I learned that drama/theater is my true passion, even in dance. Playing other characters and embellishing emotions is a part of who I am. My favorite thing to do as a child was to play house with my brother, which then turned into a dramatic sitcom with more than one hundred characters by the time I was thirteen (see chapter 17). I enjoyed playing alone too, which also consisted of embellished motions and emotions.

In fifth grade, I was bullied for being "too dramatic and weird." I was an interesting child (that's okay, not everyone needed to understand it). I have written numerous comedic plays and performed them in hospitals for years. Middle school gave me the opportunity to find my comfort in the drama club and performing in plays with people who I felt comfortable being myself with. I have been everything from princes, princesses, and fairies to mermaids and various animals. One of my best roles was in eighth grade as a crazy director who dressed in various costumes. I've never been on a professional audition, though I can definitely see myself becoming at least a tiny bit famous one day.

As you can see, drama and theater are not only therapeutic to view (movies, plays, etc.) but also to be a part of, even if it's not for a performance. I have been extensively educated on the healing properties of drama for individuals, groups, and communities. Drama helps people gain perspectives of themselves and others. I remember a former professor saying, "Drama highlights taboo conflicts of human nature; death, love/sex, and power." I always loved my acting classes and various theater exercises because they gave me the opportunity to fully let go, be silly, and be myself.

For my first day of graduate class, I was able to tell the students about myself from the perspective of my brother. It felt liberating to embody Rob's persona and throw some shade about myself. Normally, I may not have communicated my weaknesses if I was talking as myself, but my brother had no problem doing that. I found it amusing to listen to everyone's role-playing as it heightened my understanding about people and their relationships. My friend acted like me afterward, and I thought it was hilarious. This has been a game my family has played for years. Role-playing can be very useful when used in the appropriate way (to avoid feelings being hurt).

I also learned that there are different roles one can play, including fantasy, social, physiological, and cultural; each is used to achieve different outcomes. Psychodrama is a powerful form of role-playing because it is very personal; a person physically recreates personal feelings and stories. Drama interventions where psychodrama might occur have shown to be effective with various populations, even Holocaust survivors. In these situations, a facilitator is crucial in helping to provide a safe space, in addition to comfort for the individual participant(s).

I had the honor of participating in a playback theater at Lesley University. (Playback theater is a social justice aspect of psychodrama that helps people witness their stories of trauma played out and improvised in real life.) I was astounded by the true-story theater concepts and actors. At Lesley, they portrayed my story and feelings better than I could ever express it. Thinking back on it now, it is even more meaningful because I had a huge setback not long after this performance. It showed my peers the true essence of me and why I am so grateful to be here. Being a part of playback theater and continuing to practice drama is part of my life's dance.

Music

"Da, da dum, da, ba." Naturally my mind is in song, even if it's offbeat to the sounds playing around me. Some people are bothered by noise; others bother to create it so people can embrace it. Music can be compared to a museum of sounds on display for all to hear. Admission is free, and in this museum of rhythm, one creates the art with his or her own instruments, including body and voice. It never goes out of style, though the production of sound has developed throughout the years. Even rhythm is a pattern that is innate; it is in our breaths and heartbeats. Nevertheless, auditory sensations help to navigate us through the world. Even for individuals who are not able to hear, they can feel vibrations of this magic of music.

I am not a skilled musician, though music enhances my skills (such as dance), my voice, and my personality. For as long as I can remember, a major part of my life has been listening to, and creating, music. Even the closest people in my life have a huge musical connection and talent, including Jess Kalamari (see chapter 17), who is a professional musician. I enjoy making music with my body and voice as an instrument through tapping, clapping, humming, etc. I first experienced music as a therapy when I was in a pediatric physical rehabilitation hospital. From then on, I was so intrigued by the healing properties of music. The music one hears and plays evokes emotion.

Personally, there are certain songs that remind me of important people and events in my life. Every song I hear brings me to a memory that helps reaffirm who I am and where I've been. I love all types of music for different reasons, but I am drawn to types that convey powerful and positive messages. For some years, Lawrence had been seeing a music therapist every couple of weeks. I have seen a ton of improvement in his attention and vocal clarity. I also attend music therapy, and it is by far my favorite and most beneficial therapy. It builds my confidence, helps me control movements (including pitch in my voice), and allows me to be myself. In late 2019, my music therapy went virtual, and Sam (my therapist, music partner, and friend) started composing music to my lyrics. I aspire to be like music that encourages all to dance—the dance that moves people with no music.

People frequently tell me, "Keep beating to your own drum." Figuratively, this encourages me to continue expressing myself by my own unique means. In other circumstances, I ask myself, "Why is it so hard to be in sync with others?" Once, in a community drumming session, my overwhelmingness and enthusiasm spilled out complete chaos and disoriented the group as I played a floor drum with my feet flailing by my arms. I definitely can be overwhelmed by certain songs, instruments, and activities; as I get older, I'm learning to harmonize with others.

Singing and implementing musical activities in nursing homes opened my eyes to how magical music is. It's like zombies coming alive. When I worked with others, my musicality became enhanced from singing often, as I used music to increase therapeutic interventions and make people smile. Sometimes materials were low—my voice, body, a trash can, and a hospital bin were all I had as tools for a music intervention. Nonetheless, I made it work.

Drums, string instruments, and pianos captivate me, though I use my body as an instrument the best. My sporadic musical rhythms match the energetic and soulful paintings I create in fine arts.

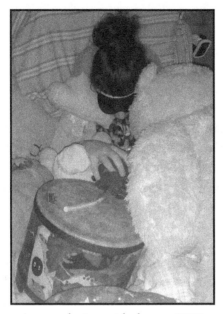

Amara playing with drums, 2020

Visual/Fine Art

When many people think of the word *art*, this is what often comes to mind: paintings, drawings, and sculptures. This type of art brings wonder to the eye. Inner images of the psyche come alive, representing life's emotions in a tangible form.

Art therapy has many principles and outcomes, whether it's for catharsis, relaxation, conflict resolution, or sensory development. I have visually seen this through working with people in various art projects. I'm always inspired by how much depth one artistic process and product can reveal about a person. Through fine arts, I realized I have a pattern of free expression, putting color on every aspect of a page. This was my style from kindergarten to now. I guess this just goes with my personality and feelings; I even dress that way. I have always loved coloring, drawing, and painting; however, my poor fine motor skills dismissed me from participating in the arts for a period of time.

Art therapy allows me to feel freedom and release from my unconscious, to splatter. I never did well in art class because I had trouble replicating certain techniques or projects. Nevertheless, I love viewing the artwork of others because it evokes emotion within myself, similar to the emotion one gets from watching a movie or hearing a song.

Although visual art can be made with almost any material, the quality of material in visual art is essential to the effectiveness. Oil and chalk pastels are my favorite materials to work with because I adore the texture. I've enjoyed having more opportunities to work with these mediums in my classes. In addition, I've also used water-color paints, which were a new medium for me. As I love water, mixing water and paint together felt very fulfilling. Clay is another one of my favorite materials because it's three-dimensional and easily changeable. Soft air-dry clay has been my favorite because the lack of coordination in my hands makes other fine arts very difficult and frustrating. Using clay has allowed me to strengthen my hands and create sculptures in the hospital.

Sensation in art is very important to creativity and the sensory experience overall. I feel that every material has its own purpose. Each form can be equally beneficial for someone, depending on his or her goal. Some individuals need to stay grounded on a smaller canvas, while others benefit from expanding to much larger surfaces. I think limiting materials can help prevent overstimulation in some cases. Other times, the ability to provide an abundance of materials enhances opportunities for emotional expression.

Visual art, like the other art forms, can also be very accessible to integrate with play, such as with sand tray therapy, which allows people expression through forming sand and mimicking their feelings to tell stories. As Leonardo da Vinci once said, "Painting is poetry that is seen rather than felt, and poetry is painting that is felt rather than seen."

Do you consider yourself an artist? Which area do you feel most comfortable in? Why? In what ways can you participate more to help yourself and others D.A.N.C.E.?

Chapter 17
Connection

Connection: "Something that joins or connects two or more things."[44]

I feel connected to…

> **The ground:** I, too, have been walked on by people.
> **People:** As we exist together on earth.
> **Earth:** As we spin, water helps me on land.
> **Water:** Because it's defied by gravity.
> **Gravity:** I fall like leaves of a tree.
> **Tree:** My inner core is sappy; thus, I still stick to it.
> **Sticks:** I will not disappear like a balloon; when I break, parts of me branch out.
> **Balloon:** I come in different forms to celebrate life, tied by my friend the ribbon.
> **Ribbon:** I have many purposes and can be cut with scissors.
> **Scissors:** I cut things out or off to create the ideal picture.
> **Picture:** I'm a memory of a moment someone has treasured.
> **Treasure:** Really not secretive—if you look to find me.
> **Secret:** Can you relate to this too? Maybe there's a hidden connection between me and you.
> **Hidden:** Nope. If you are reading this, we are made to create and bond.

As you can see, we can go on and on about what we are connected to—because it's everything! Finding relatedness in people and things opens doors to inclusion, empathy, creativity, and even optimism. This, to me, is the greatest outcome of my D.A.N.C.E. This connection is prevalent, not only on a grand scale, but in everyday life. (When I was asked which two words went together during a neurological test, I struggled because I can always describe relatability with anything. That is why the game *Apples to Apples* is my favorite.) Even in small situations, we can always look for the bigger picture.

In this generation, one may feel most connected to technology. I get it. We like to be seen, heard, and understood. Phones, computers, and other technological advances have made communication and learning more accessible. It's contradictory in some ways, though, because as it connects us to the world, it also pulls us away from it. My mom always tells stories about how much fun she had playing outside with her neighborhood friends when she was a child. This still happens in this society, but interpersonal interaction is less and less present. Video and computer games can have their benefits, but they're incomparable to physical outdoor games. Even when I was a child, technology was far less advanced than it is now. I used disposable cameras in the 2000s, then digital cameras, and now my camera is on my phone. In the professional world as well, nowadays you can get a degree, apply to a job, and get hired completely remotely. Businesses and schools carry on with face-to-face interactions solely online. The bright side is, although communication evolves drastically, we'll always have common language (of some form).

As you know, I adore language arts and cultural diversity. I think sign language in particular is one of the most beautiful languages of all, and it's one I wish I studied, even though it's not realistic for people with movement disorders. I can't stress the value and validity of this form of communication enough. Even though I don't use sign language, I'm lucky I still have a means to communicate.

People used to ask me if I spoke Italian (we do have a tendency to speak with our hands). I do know some words from my family and my high school Italian class. I also took French in middle school because I love the ballet language. In college, I even took Spanish because it's the most practical for my work, and I was around that language frequently at Kean University. Unfortunately, I never mastered any of the romantic languages despite being a hopeless romantic. I definitely could have spoken better Spanish if I practiced more.

Thankfully, there is a silver lining in all this. The thing I love about being nonverbal is that I can speak all the languages—my phone can speak any for me! (Also, they say 70 percent of communication is nonverbal. Might as well focus on the means of connection that matter most.) Even though I don't use speech as my primary form of communication, at this point, I feel more culturally connected than ever.

When I was losing my speech, some nursing aides thought I spoke Russian. I wasn't even "rush-ing." I was just trying to take my time saying yes or no. Sometimes my high-pitched, dysphonic tone even sounds Chinese. This actually makes me feel more relatable to all beings. (The ironic thing is, I remember being diagnosed with foreign accent syndrome[45] after my initial TBI. It's in my brain chart and everything.) Things have a funny way of coming back around. For a time, my responses also sounded Jamaican, as most of what would audibly come out was "Ya, man," regardless of what I was trying to say (at least, that's how it sounded). My family got a kick out of it. In a sense, I was exceptionally agreeable. We might as well call that blessing a universal expression of peace.

On One Hand...

> New hands to hold
> And discoveries to unfold
> Truths to be told
> Here we go breaking the mold
> From meek to bold
> Warming this freezing cold

I thank all those who held my hand. In my heart, I am holding it with you. It may not be the strongest grip, but I am there for you. I feel the love of all people. In my dance classes, I adopted a yoga tradition where we passed "love and a wish" around a circle. Holding hands can be germy and sweaty, but the human connection is like

145

no other. The social distancing during the coronavirus pandemic of 2020 showcases the blessings of technology to keep us connected and save lives.

> It's incredible how an individual can fight
> Helps a community unite
> And a world's battle
> Allows each individual to rattle

Hands down, love comes in handy—handling the unpredictability of the hand I've been dealt! There is nothing like being physically present with another person.

On the Other Hand...

I am grateful technology keeps me connected when I feel isolated in my disability world. It's extremely imperative to help give people with disabilities, especially those with social impairments, opportunities to interact with the outside world in any way possible. We all relate to each entity differently. The connections I have made with people, regardless of their outcomes, have created my life and this book.

It all started with my family giving me freedom and tools to make my own connections. The fact that my dad worked as a pharmacist at SUNY Downstate Hospital in Brooklyn was the reason I was able to stay there for five weeks getting royal treatment and dozens of doctors willing to tackle my complex case. Here are a couple of stories of special friends I am blessed to have come in contact with.

Connected at the Hippie Level

Do you know those people who make you feel like they share a part of your spirit? When I receive a message saying, "Hey, what's poppin', my lovie?" I know who it's from. There is one redhaired human/fairy/leprechaun/hippie like no other.

I met my incredible friend, delightful Delanie, in November of 2014 when she was a junior in high school. She had expressed interest in volunteering with Riccio Pick-Me-Ups. Her compassion radiates from her youthful, free-spirited persona. She became the hippie to my leggie. (I coined the term *leggie* for anyone still attached to some hippie generation principles, like standing up for what he or she believes in, even if that person does not stand tall physically. This is also a legging-obsessed generation. I love my cute, comfy leggings).

At each visit and fundraiser, Delanie and I were able to enhance our abilities to spread flower power, comedy, entertainment, and joy. We inspire each other, which makes us both leggies. We are the future blossoms moving forward, showing positive growth in our nations. I am so honored to connect with Lanie Love and others who share my passion for connectivity of earth and people.

Together We Have Class

Going to school, especially away to college, allowed me to expand my horizons and connect with others whom I wouldn't normally have the opportunity to interact with. Before my freshman year of college, I attended a three-day leadership retreat with other incoming freshmen who had passions for helping others. It was an amazing experience, though I was nervous. I did not immediately make friends with everyone because the group dynamic seemed a bit too cliché for me. However, I did meet two amazing, cultured, mature, and compassionate young women (Fiorella and Archeline), whom I connected with much more during the year. They were my closest friends in college, and we were ALWAYS there for one another throughout our adulting processes. Even toward senior year when things were busy, we stayed connected. My bonita, Fiorella, is now a bilingual elementary education teacher who does her best to contact and visit me. I am not sure where my other bestie is now; I'm just grateful for our special friendship and the classy, compassionate, courageous woman she is to the world.

In graduate school during July of 2017, I chose to do an online program that included a three-week residency in Cambridge,

Massachusetts. I never learned so much through classes and outside experiences than I had in those three weeks. Making friends is occasionally easy for me because I am very open and welcoming, although in groups of people, it's more difficult. On the first day and during the first twenty minutes of the program, I found my best friend for life. Usually with my best friends, I know right away, similar to the "love at first sight" principle, though it was also by sound. My best friend's name is Jessica, a.k.a. Kalamari, a beautiful, fun-loving, talented, wonderfully unique musical student from Connecticut. We felt each other's openness and passion from day 1. We bonded over music, art, adventure, and the spontaneity of living life to the fullest. I had the absolute greatest three weeks of my life in Cambridge with her as my roommate. She is the closest friend I met in my adult life thus far.

Throughout all the medical madness that happened, our friendship is still going strong. I think what makes our connection so special is, together, we connect on a greater level to things and people. Together we learn, write, sing, befriend strangers, play music, dance, make mud angels, swim, laugh obnoxiously, cry, dramatize, and vent. I'm the marinara (Maramara) to her calamari (Kalamari). In the words of Jess, "Our love may seem annoying to some, but it's pure like distilled water." The water does not run out, even when its particles get polluted; it's the finest H_2O from the deepest depth of the ocean.

Circle of Life (January 12, 2018)

Circles are my favorite shape. They do make me dizzy, going 'round and 'round, but circles are where all sight can be seen and sound heard. They unite all the love and people. They also tend to create a small world around a person's life. For me, that small, unified world is dance, health care, rehabilitation, education, and charities in my communities. One thing always leads to another (like with illnesses).

Dance had led me to the initial trauma of being hit by a car, which led me to the rehab world, which then inspired me to become a recreation therapist, which, in turn, allowed me to further my education and work. Well, life's dance has led me, once again, to the health/rehab journey. Also, I never would have imagined that one year after my internship, my former patient (Stephanie), whom I worked with last year at another facility, would speed by me in a wheelchair in the nursing facility I'm currently in for rehab.

Yes, I did see a part of *The Lion King* the other day on television. It made me tear more than usual. The way I see it is that there's a connection between life and death. What goes around comes around; history repeats itself, and God brings you back to where you are meant to be. The thirteen-year-old stubborn, impatient patient in me makes me try to overpower my mind or body, making me a risk and needing an alarm. I fall because I have a goal, and the rise has just not yet been successful.

***

Seven months after the above post was written, I attended rehabilitation at the hospital I previously interned at for five months. Being there was bittersweet because all the staff knew me (which was helpful because they have known the person I am). Furthermore, it's also upsetting because I see the looks on their faces, which attempt to hide disbelief and sadness for my condition. A blessing from all this is that I visited Stephanie a few times a month and during the holidays. My mom and I brought her on recreational experiences she otherwise would not have had the opportunities to do because of living in a nursing home and a lack of social support.

The stories she told brought me priceless amounts of joy, and her quality of life has significantly increased with our help giving her the freedom she longed for. During my five weeks as an inpatient at the facility, Stephanie and I made bracelets and played games. I passed on my beading legacy to her to share with others. There's a string of hope as long as it can loop around. It's all about connecting people, things, places, and passions. I believe we came into each other's lives for a special reason, just as all connections do in this circle of life.

Fulfillment you attain through connection isn't the kind that is necessarily fed to you by the outside world. It is a connection that comes from within; after you take away the others…the thing that binds you to your inner self; life, in its glory. (Jessica Giannone)

*Think about some of your most valued connections that were made. How has it changed your life? What and who do you feel most connected to? What do you think that says about you and life in general?

Chapter 18
Imagination

That's the real trouble with the world, too many people grow up.

—*Walt Disney*

DO YOU REMEMBER THE DAYS when you believed in figures like Santa Claus, and you thought jumping off the couch was flying and that magic really did exist? Ah, the purity of childhood imagination is made up of more than just memories to me. I know we grow older and get in touch with reality, but why does it have to socially contaminate us?

I'm blessed to have had a wonderful childhood where imagination ruled my world as I discovered the real one. I played with dolls until my early teens when no one would play with me anymore. However, I struggled emotionally when I turned sixteen, and even in my adult life I've had moments when I felt I wasn't growing up like others my age. Surprisingly, I learned that an extended childhood actually brings more maturity. It has taught me how to live in the moment, explore, believe, be confident, and discover me. My creations of childhood extended into adulthood, where they helped me decenter (deviate) from the mess in order to recenter (focus) on my message.

This little mermaid appreciates the bare necessities of having a toy story where she dreamed of being a princess in a neverland to see her true reflection and paint with all the colors of the wind. I have always been inspired by Disney, which never would have been created without one motivated man's dream of a mouse coming to life. (Before Walt Disney's career took off, he was rejected hundreds of times and told he wasn't creative enough.) Imagination bridges the impossible with an imposter that actually encourages one to believe. Thus my motto: possibilities over probabilities. Magic is always there to those who cast its spell; it just takes character.

Pages of Potential

In elementary school, I wrote stories about made-up creatures, such as grovers, using my spelling words. I loved putting my imagination on paper. In second grade, the local newspaper published a story of mine about a magical butterfly. The butterfly was my main character who helped Dave go to school (inspired by my brother Lawrence's journey to find a school that could handle his needs and appreciate his abilities). In third grade, my teacher told me I should have my own magazine. I quickly imagined it, then created *Just for Kids*, a magazine filled with games, stories, poems, recipes, jokes, and artwork by and for children in my school. My mom helped me collect submissions, copy, and distribute it because she saw the potential.

Six years later, I brought the magazine back, this time making it *For Miracles by Miracles*, giving it to anyone with a chronic illness and disability who needed a pick-me-up. It was sent by mail and distributed in hospitals. Jessica was a huge supporter as well. Eventually, it stopped, as it became too much to do mostly on my own. Then the growth of technology hindered the dream. Yet I always imagined being a writer. I never would have imagined writing in this condition. At the same time, my circumstances give me more of a story, which I'm blessed to share with you now.

Can You Play with Me?

My brother Rob and I are close in age, so we always played together. We included our older brother (Lawrence) too, but his characters in our house game were invisible, as imaginary play was not his thing. Rob was around three or four years old, and I was five years old when we started to play in our world. This house game started with a mom, a dad, and a baby, eventually growing to literally hundreds of characters and families within that decade. Playing in our world was my and my brother's favorite thing to do. We would legitimately act out these different characters in their crazy lives for hours on end, frequently with the utilization of other toys as well.

There is more than one synopsis, but the main plot consisted of a baseball player named Mario Rodriguez, his nurse wife, two identical twin girls, Jarissa and Sierra, along with three other adopted children. Mario owned a sports authority (not the store, but a recreation complex). So, in turn, we would play a variety of sports as well as attend and host Olympics, talent shows, pageants, parties, and everyday events. The characters and families dealt with real-life issues, such as disabilities, illnesses, death, poverty, divorce, and relationship conflicts.

We had fun portraying different voices and mannerisms and acting like people from numerous cultures. As soon as I turned eight years old, I even did research to make situations and people more realistic. It was our way of dealing with our own problems in a projected form of other characters, which is an element of psychodrama. After my accident, of course, a couple of characters had accidents and illnesses too. It's amazing how children use their imaginations to heal themselves without knowing it. That is why expressive therapies can be the most powerful form of healing. We would play anywhere and anytime, especially when stressed. No one in the entire universe will ever understand our world except us. I still use my imagination and continue the lives of our world. Thinking back on it now, we created something remarkable, which marked our passions for life.

Mermaid Moon
by Delanie Cosgrove

Right off Oyster Ave, under the sparkling white moon shining bright in the night sky, there is a heaven where mermaids love to dance.
Come explore the ocean floor.

*Watch in amazement as you learn to perform tricks of all
    kinds!*
The sea foam laughs, the waves cartwheel.
*The water floats you to paradise where the trees happily parade
    around the island using their branches as drumsticks
    and their bark as the drum.*
*The sand joins the parade of cheerfulness as they shake their
    maracas to the beat of "We Will Rock You" by Queen!*
*The wind plays the percussion perfectly. It's really quite a
    unique quest.*
Come take a chance, and let your fin prance.
Let your hair loose and your smile ooze.
*Open your heart's belief in the magic of the white moon smil-
    ing down on you as you dive to the depths of the sea.*
There's so much to see; just open your eyes of wonder.
*Fishes as orange as a tangerine with scales as yellow as the sun-
    shine. Starfishes as pink as the sunset. Whales as blue as
    the clear sky on the sunniest of smiliest days.*
*Just trust the water. The water will always be there to guide
    your heart to find that the treasure is within you. You
    are a treasure chest filled with the most captivating
    jewels.*
*Your soul is the bracelet of charm, wearing your heart on your
    arm; bringing love to everyone you swim with aside the
    sunlit zone.*
*You are a mermaid of mesmerizing melodies. Won't you please
    take a chance and allow the moon to be your partner
    in dance?*

***Have you ever had an imaginary friend or character in your
life who just seemed to go away as you became older? What would
they be like now? How do you think imaginative play helped you
during that period of your life?**

Chapter 19
Personal Creations

The best way to learn about something is to travel the depths of the "C."

CREATING FOR (AND WITH) OTHERS is transformative because it ties in with the entire D.A.N.C.E. process. In this chapter, I wanted to share some artistic pieces that stand out to me.

One of my strengths (and weaknesses) is cherishing all people and places with all my heart. This helps me to love, but it makes it harder for me to lose. Apparently, I need to learn lessons from Princess Elsa to just let it go. When I came home in August of 2017 from my graduate school experience, just months before my new illness, I unexpectedly found out I was getting my room repainted and redecorated. I needed to decide what had to be thrown out, donated, or put away. Ironically, after about eight months, my room was then moved downstairs in order to be accessible for my new abilities. I never imagined the prior cleansing of past treasures would be a helpful tool on a deeper level down the road.

I have many treasures from my childhood, which were acquired before and during the life-changing experiences from my accident. These objects are symbolic of my life's journey and progress, and they have fragmented down throughout the years. Even though the pieces are worn out or broken, they are beautiful to me. Therefore, I decided to take the broken pieces of my childhood treasures to the present and create a sculpture. This process took me several hours for several days, and it's still a work in progress. The initial process was extraordinary because everything kept falling. I did not give up.

I used glue and duct tape, and I tried out different formations. It reminded me of my life.

I feel off-balance, I fall and rise, yet I have a strong support system. Fittingly, I had to change the base support of my sculpture in order for it to be steady. It does not stand as tall and sturdy as I dreamed, but it's dynamic, creative, and meaningful like me!

The focal piece is my old, broken iPod that helped me through sleepless nights in the hospital. I glued on sentences from an essay I wrote in seventh grade one month before my accident named "Why Me? Why Not?" These words resonated with me throughout my recovery and still inspire me today. Some of the artwork was given to me handmade by special friends and family. I cut the "Creative Connection" label from a Dr. Natalie Rodgers book because her principles embody my life, and she is a huge influential figure in the expressive arts field. After I made the sculpture, I wrote the following poem, which I also read aloud several times to enhance the creative experience.

I used a psychotherapy[46] technique where I spoke about my experiences through a narrative of artwork using "I am."

> I am here, I am here
> But part of me is broken
> That is my fear
> Of just becoming a past token
>
> I am the...
> Music that once played
> Powerful words that were written
> Dancer that tumbled and slayed
> Colorful flower power kitten
>
> I am the...
> Hot glue that holds the sculpture together
> With the duct tape that masks the empty places
> Inspiring the spirit to fly with the purple feather
> To put color and wonder in all places

I am…
Guided by the angels and a heavenly dove
With support from family, friends, and the grounds below
Each creation handmade with love
Crafted on the flowerpot allowing the flowers to grow

I am…
The "peace(s)" of the puzzle and pie
Figuring out the game while enjoying each slice
The off-balance structure who contradicts the "why?"
The rocks, beads, and baskets that sacrifice

Their individuality to come to create
A bigger picture work of art
Displaying its beauty before it's too late
Why not? I am the start

Of the already begun
The movement; the dance
To the inspiring songs sung

I am…
Here, ready for my chance

I am…
Abstract, Anomalous, Attuned

I am ME: AmArA

Punspirations (January 17, 2018)

Have you ever felt like an animal? I feel like a cat. I feel like I'm constantly coughing up hairballs. My goal is to be independent. I'm still confident in myself, but I want to just sleep and get warm. I am like a cat living in a turtle's shell.

More than two months ago, I wrote the following punny cat poem to express thoughts about growing up and gaining indepen-DANCE. I painted a picture of a cat who had one eye, and I was inspired by my new kitty who always went on my shoulder.

> What is it like to grow older?
> Hmm, feeling a KITten on my shoulder
>
> Not fitting in a CATegory or sKIT
> Or being told when to sCAT or sit
>
> Depending on them or I
> A CATerpillar turns into a butterfly
>
> Having a CATaract-blurred lens
> With sensitive ears and a voice that sends
>
> Raspy sounds through a CAThartic dance
> Moving after a CATatonic trance
>
> Cooking in the KITchen brings the heat
> This CATalog is incomplete
>
> Independence KIT: fluid and free
> Achieved by more than solely me
>
> A KIT-CAT: some chocolate, some crunch
> Made by a bunch (of cocoa)
>
> Because I'm cuckoo but I really don't know
> What is it like to grow?

Art Inspired by Color (May 12, 2018)

For the past two months, I had a goal of performing at yesterday's Paint the Mall Purple event for Mental Health & Recovery

Awareness Day, and I made it! It felt MAGICAL. The presentation and dance went better than imagined because I was surrounded by a wonderful crowd; my parents, friends, mutual friends, the beautiful organization CFC Loud N Clear, and strangers coming together. I proved to myself, despite this craziness, I still got it!

In expressive dance, it doesn't matter about strength or controlled movement, so it was perfect. Even people on the second floor were watching and dancing along too. The tears of joy and love were indescribable.

Yesterday was my first night out doing my thang since our November 11 gala. It was difficult sleeping before and after. My brain and body were shaken up. I am able to rise up like I did yesterday because of all my loves.

In lieu of rising up…

Purple was my first word, is my favorite color, and represents the crown chakra; pure thought…

> Do I really need to get out of bed?
> I'm feeling the rage of red
>
> I'm sad and sleepy, feeling blue
> I know I can get up being bold and true!
>
> Yes, yes, let's do this!
> Mix these together showing royalty
> Luxury of lilac and lavender loyalty
>
> Having genuine loved ones is the best
> Passion of periwinkle takes care of the rest
>
> After the storm of life there's a rainbow
> Tied with light there to show
>
> There's always hope, even the violet
> It's a natural happening, I cannot regret

The choices I made to make it here
I am who I am, living with faith over fear

So mauve, magenta, amethyst, plum, and grape
Thank you, purple, for taking shape

In the earth, objects, and inside me too
I think I will wake up with red and blue

Creating positivity, purple gives me a chance
To live, laugh, love, and DANCE

Amara enjoying dancing to the song "Rise Up" with
friends; high school bestie Ilana holding her hand

Breathe from Black to Gold

For our 2016 talent show fundraiser, I wrote this poem, which
was inspired by the people we met in hospitals. Specifically, a boy
named Thomas whom we became close to passed away around this

time. I recorded the following poem as a dramatic spoken word, then I danced to its recording wearing my friend's black-and-gold dance dress. At the end of the performance, I brought up six kids to tie together the theme of unity to the song "We Can Be Heroes," Thomas's favorite song. This was one of my most powerful interdisciplinary pieces.

(sounds of breathing)
I slowly walk into a room with walls of an awkward white
Beep, beep, beep...I'm watching a child in fight of his life

The air is filled a charcoal black
As internal monsters are on the attack

Heroes are fighting rarities
Families dealing with disparities
Getting no clarities!
Ahhhhh!

I was that child lying in the bed
With fractures, bruises, and bleeding in my head

Leaving me semi-paralyzed, petrified
How do I conceptualize?

Life brand new
What do I do?

Years of my recovery
Led to my discovery

Beauty to breathe gold

The happiness of yellow chicness
Uniqueness

Of metallic brown
The color I get when the world is turned upside down

Leaving you on your side
For a roller-coaster ride

Turning and turning
Yearning…
For love
Brought by those up above

When we breathe together
We defy forces lighter than a feather

I still shiver in cold
Have to do what I'm told
I learn to be bold

It's you who inspires me
When in life I'm tired to see

In a sea of waves seemingly strange
We have to be the change

You know…
Give a pick-me-up, help those fighting hard…breathing
from black to gold…

***

There is a cliché saying that the best gifts come from the heart. Things are better when they're handmade. I gained a passion for art because I realized how much art impacts people, despite how perfect works come out. This started my nonprofit movement. It's the amount of time, love, emotion, and energy one puts into art that makes it priceless. Something as simple as a card, painting, bracelet, or small sculpture can make a huge difference in someone's life. Everything can have a special, symbolic meaning, which a person can cherish forever, embracing each connection in life's D.A.N.C.E.

> *If I can fly in my way and not listen to what they say about how hopeless or bad it could be, then you can make a song—at first, maybe wrong—but do not be embarrassed in front of me. (Ilana Klein)*

Ilana is my incredibly talented and kind high school best friend who wrote and illustrated the most beautiful book, *Two Little Birds*, about our friendship for my twenty-first birthday. We take pride in using our creativity to cherish our friendship. The best gifts are from the heart, and this is the greatest gift given to me by a friend. Lana Bird and I have had such amazing memories together. In December of my sophomore year, I took my usual stroll to the nurse's office with my paraprofessional. I was in a wheelchair, mostly for safety, as I was still very off-balance with walking due to hemiparesis[47] from the TBI. When I arrived, a local radio station was playing my story (for WOBM's "Making Miracles Radiothon") to benefit the Children's Specialized Hospital Foundation. I met a very friendly girl who was there in the office for a cold. We started talking and bonded over our love of performing arts. She was in the specialized acting program. Then I found out her birthday is the same day as the anniversary of my accident.

I did not see or talk to Ilana until a year after I met her. I only found her name on social media through a mutual friend. After this, we started a long, beautiful history of everyday lunches senior year, hangouts, celebrations, volunteering, performances, fundraisers, sleepovers, and being there for each other through it all. The impact she has had on my life is what makes her so special to me. Her ability to accept not only my family and I, but herself and all others, has made all the difference. Her efforts led her to work with special populations in a variety of settings, as well as to pursue theatrical passions. She continues to inspire me. Sometimes we fly our separate ways—always coming back, singing with oodles and oodles of love, our song for all to hear.

Thanksgiving Eve (November 22, 2017)

Gratitude snuggles me in my sleeve

Warming the cold shiver
Always unpredictable about what life delivers

I am thankful that…

I can paint a picture my voice cannot convey
Beauty and wonder overpower even when I feel dismay

All the dimensions of life are sensational
Sending sporadic hope that's rotational

For the love of one another
All my sisters, brothers, father, and mother

The rainbows appear after it rains
The water on earth that remains

Recently, I am reminded just how amazing life is. Changes always happened, but butterflies show change is beautiful. This Thanksgiving, I'm grateful for the changes, regardless for what it is. God helps us to be fearless, fearing less, but yes, there is still fear. May God bless all this season, filling faith through fear. Wishing as much health and happiness as possible.

Grateful to be home with my family, never taking anything for granted, blooming from where we are planted.

Do you ever create something to express just for your personal well-being or create for others? Both are important for creative nourishment of the whole self.

Part 5
Embrace

The indescribable feeling of a hug; feeling safe, warm, and snug

Feeling supported, loved, appreciated, and celebrated

Holding on to one another; mother, sister, brother

It's a gorgeous grace; each place and face—we must embrace

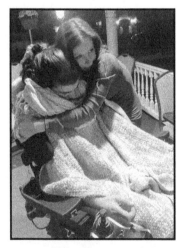

Amara and Jessica, November 2019

As WE WALK AND ROLL on this journey together, the discoveries, accomplishments, nourishments, and creations need to be felt, recognized, and celebrated in order to complete the D.A.N.C.E. process. Each moment is a gift we continue to unwrap. The gifts last forever in spirit, but not in body. The value of life is understood by the understanding of death. The truth is, we never know what is going to happen next. Some people appreciate life on a different level, like myself, because experiences constantly threaten the livelihood of ourselves and close loved ones.

Fear of the future is inevitable, though it's crucial to remind ourselves we are here now. We live for the ones who came before, with, and after us. I feel compelled to touch the world that touched me. I'm talking about a safe, gentle, therapeutic touch that spreads genuine love. Due to my condition, I have not been able to merely hold someone again without my arms flailing. I learned how to embrace it all with my strongest senses, bracing myself in a way that's sensational.

Chapter 20
The Journey

Journey: "Something suggesting travel or passage from one place to another"[48]

When will the journey be adjourned? Is this a court case? We wait and anticipate. The case is never closed, even when it's gone.

IMAGINE BEING ON A COUNTRY road in the dark with hills that go up, down, then up again. There is no map, cell phone service, or indication of any person around to ask for directions. This happened to my family when we were lost while driving in Pennsylvania. I compared this scary encounter to the journey of life.

Eventually, we made it to our destination after we took a new route, discovering new beauties unplanned for. Sometimes we never wound up where we thought we wanted to go. It was still worth it.

Journeys like this seem endless. We are born with a destination through our parents who have their own journeys. Then we grow up having our personal journeys as we plan for the next up to achieve those dreams we set. The process and in-between moments are the greatest parts of life's D.A.N.C.E. Learning the steps, falling, making mistakes, changing choreography, and experimenting are the parts of the dance that are more rewarding than the performance itself. The journey can be ruthless, seemingly never-ending. Sometimes I just want to know what the future holds. Each day I am learning to just hold on to today, embracing the journey. Throughout the dances, the country drives, and all the adventures, I became a stronger, more cultured individual.

The journey eventually needs to come to an end. Even when writing, we express many statements with commas and even semi-colons. Eventually it all ends. We do not know when, but death is a given. My mom always reminds me, "The only definite things in life are death and taxes." In many religions like my own, dying is just the beginning of a new life, even if it's not on this physical earth.

I have gone through a near-death experience, been there with others during their last breaths, spoken to grieving individuals, and sometimes, the concept of a journey is too large to grasp. Funerals just feel too somber, so a decided preference for someone like myself would be a celebration of life. I wrote a paper on complex grief and traumatic deaths as my final paper before becoming sick. I think grieving the death of another can often be more difficult than the act of death for an individual. The death of one kills parts of many. People like to talk and reason, but sometimes there are no reasons, unless we create our own.

Questioning her own grief, my cousin Jessica wrote a column in dedication of Uncle Neil, and I wanted to include an edited excerpt:

> *I do believe in the value of understanding; aware-ness and knowledge as tools for healing. Anxiety and its crew will ultimately join the grieving party, along with all the other natural "defense" mecha-nisms. But they're just side effects of the journey. And there is no true destination. I think that's the point.*
>
> *You want to know why we go "crazy" when things vanish from our lives? Not because we think we can't live without them. Or the pain of missing them consumes our consciousness. Or we're afraid we'll never fill that hole again.*
>
> *It's because we are primitive beings. We are, by nature, existing at a constant; a consistent rate in time and space where the world keeps on moving, leaving us to live in this unremitting pattern.*

When something changes, that pattern is threatened, and we habitually react. It's not so much insanity as it is a survival instinct—kicking in to tell us that we have been thrown off the constant, and we have to once again become one with our own life; a life that is no one else's, and a life that keeps on going...

Our emotions kick in, our mind takes over, and it signals the distress of a fluke in our comfortable pattern. But it is our mind that also has the capacity to continue going; moreover, to try to change for the better.

The only thing that takes us away from the static, pacing world is this entirely new mentality; carrying on as its own force—one that surpasses all else at its own rate, and one that will never, ironically, be bound to anything else.

It is free.

Typically, there are no classes you can take that teach you about life while also teaching about death. This was actually part of my journey. I feel privileged to have taken the nationally recognized Death in Perspective class by Dr. Norma Bowe at Kean University, which has a three-year waiting list for a reason. Dr. Bowe's mission and education highlights the human experience of the dark lows: dying and grieving those who died. She has helped me open up the rawness inside of me along with increasing my interest in working with people who are dying and/or have lost a loved one. My professor is fearless in her work and has inspired those around her to make a change through the organization Be the Change NJ, which values service, community, and activism.

Some of the most riveting experiences in the class were field trips to places such as cemeteries, funeral homes, hospice centers, and facilities where you can watch autopsies being performed. Each week, a personal journal assignment was shared with the class. The vibe felt more like a support group than a class at times, but that's what made it so unique. One time I even had a panic attack because another student's intense sadness transferred to me. I knew the only way out of it was to embrace the feels and let go. I literally just stood up and started screaming, throwing my book, rolling on the ground, and encouraging all to do the same. They did join me (obviously I still acted the craziest), and after a few minutes, I recollected myself.

Dr. Bowe encouraged my expression, whereas in other classes, I would have just left the room and had a full meltdown. Our assignments were truly profound, including writing our own obituaries, goodbye letters, and letters to our younger selves. I wrote most of mine in poetry format, including my "Iron and Steel" assignment below.

What's the difference between iron and steel?
Iron supplies the earth, but steel is made with fire; this
    element is real

It's stronger; that's how our railroads were built
These elements are the cabooses to helping us stand tall
    like a stilt

The fire radiates heat, burning something and making it
    melt away
It gives a light, then turns black; with light coming back
    one day

Coming back more powerful than ever
Turning those moments into a great endeavor

So some may say that my life's fire was my accident
Yes, but my experiences in hospitals would seem evident

But no, it takes more than one match of fire to burn into
    stone
For my fire was shown in each moment I felt severely sick,
    in pain, helpless, or alone

This Is Why I D.A.N.C.E.

I have trouble choosing one experience that is the worst
    or the best
Maybe it can be defined by a feeling of your heart coming
    out of your chest

Or the struggle to be someone you just are not
Fighting to appreciate the life you got

Sometimes the worst moments for me are watching my
    older brother become stuck
In his psychosis and not knowing what to do, or how to
    get him out of the muck

Thinking of the safety of my family at age 11, I learned it's
    OK to call 9-1-1
Even if the hospital placements are the opposite of fun

My fire was also in eighth grade when being my old self
    was my only yearn
Or in my early high school years when I felt like there was
    no one or nowhere to turn

When I felt powerless, letting my body and brain take
    control
Not knowing my true power was to be unstoppable

I felt guilty because I was in an out-of-state hospital, and
    my brother was moved to a group home
But then I realized he's 100 percent a part of the family
    water, providing bubbly foam

For all those moments, my brain was flooded in thoughts
    or sometimes completely blank
For all these moments, there's always someone to thank

People come and go, but my family has always been there
    helping my fire ignite
Meeting other everyday warriors, helping me through each
    fight

My mamma definitely being the biggest influence gives me
    strength to believe
My amazing therapists and supportive doctors help me
    achieve

My functional goals and beyond, never giving up on me
To the friends I made in high school through my fires,
    liking me just as I be

Even those most regretful moments of hitting my school
    aides or throwing yogurt on my head
Screaming and crying almost every night in my bed

My cousin Jessica and my best friends are my biggest sup-
    port; just one call
They help me feel better, laugh, and make sense of it all

My Dad, Rob, and Lawrence are always there to make me
    smile
So thankful for these men pushing me the extra mile

I wrote this without a central idea or direction
Just let my emotions flow as my mind gave a reflection

I know I have been through fire, but I just feel so happy
    now
The pain is a reminder I'm alive, but watching others char,
    scorch, or rot makes me go "WOW"

It hurts me more to watch others, especially those without
    support, struggling in pain

I do my best to reach out, be there for them, and just dance
    with (or for) them in the rain

Dancing…dancing…no matter how wet I may get
Soaked up, dripping in water because water helps put out
    flames

Of that fire that makes steel; life's picture frames

Capturing the essence of iron, naturally pure with fire, is
    the cure
Because yes, magic will cause smoke and incinerate, even
    risking death
But it's needed to become as strong as steel; it quantifies
    the value of each new breath

What's your iron and steel?

A year after this class, when I thought most of my fires were put
out, it came again. Luckily, my family and I had enough steel to stay
strong. I needed to constantly remind myself of that.

> *One must still have chaos in oneself to be able to give*
> *birth to a dancing star. (Friedrich Nietzsche)*

Fire (February 1, 2018)

It starts slow, then it bursts
Smoke and flames look like the worst
But there's no one to blame
We still feel such shame
The souls made it out OK
That is what matters anyway

You never know what is burning up in someone else's life, even
when the heat seems harmless. I have been upset with my brother

Rob because he has not reached out to me much through this journey. I know he is a busy senior in college. Although he is very sociable, he is so stressed. Then today, he expressed his fear of a horrible event. His whole fraternity house burned down due to an electrical fire. This is a house he worked all summer on purchasing for himself and his brothers. Everyone is safe, thank goodness! I know everything will work out for him and his friends during this distressing time.

***

Everything did work out. At the time of the above post, in the nursing home rehab, I was burning on the inside with an undiagnosed cerebellar ataxia disorder, gastroesophageal reflux,[49] vitamin deficiencies, and an autoimmune thyroid condition.[50] A couple of months later, this particular journey seemed a little more hopeful. Instead of being in a fire, I was on a train.

TRAINing 4 Life (April 17, 2018)

"I think I can, I think I can"—*The Little Engine That Could*

Every day feels like I'm on a TRAIN
With so many stops on my brain
TRAINing to get on track
Everything's like being on the attack
I have passengers and a caboose
To help when my body gets all loose
It's slow and it creaks
It's scenic and we see peaks
TRAINing when it's raining
Gaining strength
TRAINing for length

174

People say "work hard, play hard," but for people and families like myself, it's like you have to work hard just to play soft to do basic things. Everything is training and retraining in this new life (physically and mentally).

My mother had twenty-four hours' worth of training in order to take care of me. I feel bad because sometimes my legs slip under me without me knowing. Today marks four months since I was at the Jersey Shore Hospital ER. The same day, I was almost discharged. I knew something crazy was going on, but I did not expect this. I was dehydrated, anxious, out of breath, walked slowly and off-balance (independently), and struggled to swallow (still able too). I knew it was time to take that medical train, though I knew it would be a while before I got off. The four or five expected days turned into months. Training...

My mom took a train back from Florida this summer because she did not like the plane ride on the way there. I had some unforgettable train moments in New York City and Boston this summer as well. It takes so much longer journeying by train, yet time still flies, so we just try to have fun. The people you meet and the lessons you learn along the way are astounding.

Since my initial stay at the hospital, thankfully I'm experiencing more painting than pain—always training, gaining forever.

>Knowledge
>Love
>Patience
>Endurance
>Hope...

Every task and moment involve training for the next. It's exhausting because enjoyment needs to be there too. That's why more than one person and part combine to make a train run. Chugga, chugga, choo choo—choosing to TRAIN.

***

I'm still training with fire that helps ignite the fight on this journey. I have always been one to plan. I like being spontaneous when I plan to be. I just learned to go with the flow of this flower power life that has ever-changing soil.

> If plan A doesn't work, the alphabet has 25 more letters. (Claire Cook)

On this endless track, I lost count of what letter I was on; first it was *F*, now it's *G*—God's plan. Actually, I just use all the letters and numbers now. Living it up—twenty-two—wherever that leads, I learned to just FEEL it!

Em-Brace Yourself *(Cousin Jessica's Take on Our Journey from My Perspective)*

As you know, my cousin Jessica and I have been through a lot together. Despite the struggles we have shared in this journey, we're constantly reminiscing.

We have so many unforgettable memories, but one instance that serves as a typical example of our goofy experiences is our spirited New York debacle. (Manhattan is the convenient halfway mark of our locations, but not necessarily the most convenient for a pair like us to maneuver under certain circumstances.)

On this frantic occasion, I had a walking cane, and we were in a rush to get to a Cirque du Soleil show from Koreatown (barely anyone speaks English there—it's literally like a foreign country). This journey was a true test of our wills. After broken shoes, unusual cuisine, confusing bus and subway rides, and one unhelpful cop confrontation later, we willingly paid the Uber driver extra money for being loud on the lengthy drive back to Kean University that night. (We did make it to the show, of course.)

Every time I went to the city, I would feel bad for the homeless, and Jessica would unsuccessfully try to console me but end up caving to pass out care packages with me on the way to wherever we were headed. The night usually ended in a dance session/sleepover. In any case, we never had to conceal the music within us.

We've had crazy nights roaming about, dancing in cities as well. A man from Manhattan's Little Italy would serenade us outside of a restaurant while we swung around. We'd break out in silly moves in various novelty shops. We'd hop to the beat of live music on Block Island. Bounce about in Disney World in our matching visors. What's odd is that on all these occasions, we experienced numerous inconveniences and confusing halts that would throw us off the path, yet we danced.

It…A Family Update and Poem (August 24, 2019)

Wow! I'm lying here in bed not very comfortable, as usual, yet it is dark and quiet—giving me such peace. My family is at a family reunion, so I did get to see my sister Jessica earlier. I got in my chair twice this week; one time to go to the doctor to get a prescription refilled. The whole chair and postural situation is still a mess, however, a new headpiece was ordered. Being on Keppra[51] has helped my body to not have myoclonus electric shock movements as frequently. I have been suctioning more, due to dysphagia[52] making me feel clogged, aspirating. It gives me energy, refills me with air, and gets things out. So my bladder and even bowels aren't having trouble getting things out these days; a warning would be nice.

My favorite therapists (Sam for music and Casey for recreation) fill my week with immense happiness knowing I still have many abilities. My parents are busy looking at new homes and work programs for Lawrence. The programs seem to be much more organized and health-focused, which Lawrence needs.

My dad is looking for a new job. Unfortunately, the hospital and the pharmaceutical company my dad works for are disconnecting. I know my dad will find a job and spread his greatness somewhere else. It's bittersweet, as I volunteered for numerous events and days at that Brooklyn hospital, along with being hospitalized thirty-three days last year. I'll never forget how hard the doctors fought to find me a diagnosis and give treatment. However, illnesses like this take time to see how they evolve. Recently, social media, television programming, and crowdsourcing are bringing awareness to those with undiagnosed conditions.

Here is a poem I call It.

It
Changes and rearranges everything
Keeps me up at night
But I need to fight
It...to stay awake

Motivates me to create and meditate

It
Is not easy to write about
Or read it
But it is real
I will admit
It makes me feel
Shame and doubt

It
Is nameless
Certainly not famous
Barely a thing
But it is many things
And leaves me questioning
Do I want to risk
Everything for it?
To find it and grind it?
It impacts everyone
And everything

It
I need my mind

It is legit taking hold
Of me slowly...truth
Will unfold it
Can you still see me?
Hear me behind its
Systematic control?

It
I know but I don't
Want to let it go
Accept it
But I won't
With the choking
I am not joking
Intoxicating; it's frustrating
Sometimes I want to
Yet I won't let it win

It
Whatever and
wherever it takes
Us down...it's all
Meaningful
Not a second to waste
With all the commotion
And emotion

It
Better, whether it chooses to stay
You and I still have today
Yeah, all the shifts and shakes
Sometimes aches
Just reminiscing, missing, and wishing
BUT butterflies and faith
Give me a chance to D.A.N.C.E.

So yeah, it's a team effort, and day by day, I am just living and loving the best I can. Please pray for strength and peace for all those living with chronic, progressive, misunderstood, debilitating illnesses. I am not alone, and as always, thanks for your continuing support. Time to reposition and suction.

Goodnight and God bless.

What journeys have you been on? How do you think acceptance can help you move forward in this unpredictable life?

Chapter 21
The Feels

Without the most intense feelings, we wouldn't be experiencing life purely, or growing and changing on significant levels; never mind on basic levels that make us who we are. Emotions are what spark change and progress in the world because they provide the necessary, passionate push. It's the deepest feelings that are the catalysts for the biggest impacts.
—Jessica Giannone

FEELINGS, LIKE GHOSTS, ARE INVISIBLE things that can haunt and/or bless us. We cannot escape them. Instead, we can escort them to a visible place within ourselves. Contrarily, robots are programmed to complete notions and motions, yet they are senseless. That is why I believe living things are sensa-tional.

"You are so emotional, too sensitive, and why so touchy-feely?" Women are often told this. Maybe this is why our overall life spans are longer. I always thought to myself, "Aren't humans supposed to feel?" We do not have to be artists to embrace feelings. If we accept the objective (what is occurring), then we can be subjective about how we actually feel. For example, air pounds against one little spot on my leg where my blanket is not covering it (what is occurring). This makes me feel freezing cold, frustrated, and upset because I need assistance to get the blanket on my leg. It can be easy to feel overwhelmed, but I have to express what I'm going through in order to deal with the problem efficiently. This is why, in conflict resolution, it's important to use "I feel/felt" statements.

We are always affected by the things that surround us. Physical touch helps us understand the environment around us, and emotional touch helps us figure out our internal stimuli, also helping us to alter the external environment. My favorite type of thing to feel is an animal; it's truly pawsome. The soft fur mixed with a purr or lick elicits even more pleasant emotions within.

As a child, did you love touching objects and playing with sensory items such as Play-Doh, slime, squishy toys, and even shaving cream? I was (and still am) that child who loves to touch new things. That's one reason why art is one of my favorite things to partake in.

> The feeling of wind in my hair
> Tickles my face so bare
> Like my kitty's comforting wet nose
> And ooh, that silk petal of a rose
>
> Being surrounded by water in a pool
> Floating and keeping cool
> On muscles and skin
> Buoyancy feels like I have a fin
>
> Finished; a feeling untouched
> Where done is just a touch
> As long as our heart has a beat
> Senses never complete

Though my movement is impaired, I'm grateful I can still feel, unlike people with complete spinal cord injuries. People who have antisocial personality disorder cannot emotionally feel. Having different sensory or neurological disorders also alters these abilities as well. This is why pain can be a blessing. It reminds me to brace myself and embrace the fact that I'm still alive. Alive is feeling it all—the *ew*, *ooh*, *ah*, and *ha-ha*.

Here is a three-week poetry journal I started on December 6, 2017, in the beginning of my journey. I started this for my counseling session and continued it in the hospital. It represents my raw emotions from what I was feeling at the time. This is part of my "real in the feel, express or depress" movement.

Magic

The trick continues; illusion is failing
I'm a success story; a magician. Why does the world hear
  me wailing?

There's no abracadabra
Just the rawest form of Amara

No time to thaw
She knows her law

Law of attraction
Love receives a lovely reaction

When healing the self, the self heals
Feeling the self, the self feels

So she drinks hot tea with lemon to help aid…
Her body, mind, and soul because when life gives her lem-
  ons, she lets bitterness fade

Sweet warmth; a cleanse
Freezing like an icicle. Mind flexes; body struggles to bend

Nothing is stopping, so neither is she
The I (eye) that is me has more to see

The body that moves to the beat
Smiles and strength over stiffness. Ground shaking beneath
  my feet

My voice breaks
But my young ones can see my face
Ready for the highest stakes

When the music stops
They learn to keep dancing. No time to go to the tippy top

Show is already in swing
Go shake the groove thing
We keep moving

Isolate; contract
Liberate impact

Grooving
Moving…keep moving…

I'm still alive
Dancing allows me to strive

I can't help but feel as though I'm just here
Will the condition just disappear?
I am filled with faith and some fear

How can I overcome if I don't know what I'm coming over?

Mind over matter
Sky over latter

Climbing…forever…
Is that my endeavor?

Legacy leaving rise from fall
I am always ready to answer God's call

December 11

So I wear
Layers and layers so cold
Chest is full but heart is too
When will this unfold?
But the spirit always remains true

Will I strip down to the bone?
Questioning…makes me question
Is there a thing such as an answer alone?

I just keep writing to make things right

I'm becoming inspired to believe I got this
I just want to be heard; understood
Uttering all the "phonia,"[53] "phagia,"[54] "arthria"[55] dis
Feeling whole like I should

So I have my girls and my guys
To pick me up when I'm down
Honest, friendly love; no lies
We turn each other's lives around

I have the power to still give
Life can be more exciting the more we fight
That's what it means to live!
Darkness is just another shade of light

Both shades give beautiful emphasis on "be"
It stings but brings sweet honey

Because my cousin says the word "hun"
Meaning an extraordinary special one

As a child, bullies called me a spaz
No, that's my life…all that jazz

Some blues but lots of pop
I bring that contemporary in hip-hop

December 16

So here I am just trying to ensure…
I stay afloat for holidays. Faith is the only cure

That came in tears at mass
Lord told me I needed help
This condition would just pass
And that was heard in my yelp

Trouble swallowing even water or spit
Time to go to emergency "C" so it's not emergency "T"
Tragic, no; just need it

My roommate is 83
Ready to die, I hear her scream
And cry; they're killing us
She shouts "I can't take this"
Is this a dream?

Meanwhile I'm left alone in a sterile hallway
Strapped to a gurney; oh, what a journey
I fell in the bathroom too but I'm OK

I do feel pressure
Did I just deteriorate from yesterday?
While resting, my oxygen is great
With various pressures
Of my blood, but good vitals I appreciate
Living life in merry measures

Because we must measure the merry pleasures When the
    weight of the body goes down

'Cause on the eve of eve
I remember to believe
Miracles not seen in a mirror
Called from a secret reflection
Lots of introspection

I thought the music would be uplifting
I danced in my bed...still got swag
But then I was gasping and shifting
Down in bed with coughs and gags

One week ago, I thought I was a little sick
At least I danced standing up with a friend
My body is playing a trick
Only God knows when it will end

I'm breathing on my own
But need help for other skills
I let my abilities be shown
It won't be too long until

I am more like me
But hey, in most ways I'm the same
Amara Riccio; how I love my name

So on the day I miss the seven fishes
The night before Jesus was born
I swim in the sea of prayers and wishes
With my pajamas loosely worn

I went down 20 pounds
In a few weeks

Hearing more sounds
Of heartbeats

I need the weight put on my body
Not on my shoulder because that's shrinking
I'm feeling way older
Even in my wise thinking
And I wait

So as I begin this Christmas I have hope
Mary and Joseph did not give up

They found a manger
To birth their miracle boy
Sometimes things work better if they're stranger
Look at all the earth's joy

For Christmas I received the greatest gift
Love in company and things
It hurts to sit up but family gives me a lift
Such joy and exhaustion life brings

My brothers can be a pain in the neck
Make me say "What the heck"

But we're always there for loss and win
Through thick and thin

I got an infection in my tongue
But wait, they say my tongue's infectious
Smile is precious

So I swish and spit…almost got it back to pink
Every part affects another; hmm…makes me think

In the words of Amara: One of the last pictures I have standing is with my most caring uncle, Frankie, on December 21, 2017. Less than three years later, he passed away from Amyotrophic Lateral Sclerosis (ALS). Rest in peace.

December 26

I went to bed early, which worked out
I just wanted to get sleep…please
Then I got a new roommate at 3:30…about
She broke her foot really bad; such unease

I hope that we both get back on our toes
In my chronic and her acute recovery
Oh, the unpredictability of how wind blows
Ready for the next discovery

Ugh, this has been such a struggle
I just want to get warm and snuggle

I am yearning for control
Of muscles fighting so hard
With my mind and soul
Somehow this is now my card

Not the sick or disabled one
But one to fight and write in
There's too much to be done
And strength within

I am working hard to keep my ambition
Have to make hard decisions
I think the first step is proper nutrition

Third feeding tube tomorrow being placed
It's been so hard to swallow
All the substances and moments faced
Need nourishment to fill the hollow

Life is changing and rearranging
Weird and strange
But there's that little girl who sang
To me and did her dancing thang

Making me so emotional
Filled a piece of my soul

She wore a shirt that says "girls can"
I need that reminder now and then

Because God only knows what's next
My sister-cousin (and clown) "nose" how to have "hun
        pun" fun
Our humor is uniquely simple, yet complex

It took my mind off pain
I was groggy and didn't even feel a poke
And company keeps me sane
Uplifts me with a joke

So now I'm getting fed through the belly
It feels weird but I can (and will) tolerate
So one day I'll jam like the jelly
Food for thought; I compensate

December 29

Finally, after 13 days, I made it out of the hospital
Transported to a car by my unforgettable patient care tech-
      nician/flirt, Carlos
A beautiful feeling in the car showed me things are possible
Then I made it to a place that appreciates my worth

They treat me like a queen
But is this what I need?

I need my crown raised high
Not just acknowledged by

Still waiting…some things never change, and it's still hard
      to coin its sense (cents)
Insurance just wants a pretty penny
Even though we give them plenty

January 1

A new year; same frustrations
Time to fight

Amara Riccio

At least the 101-year-old woman at the nursing station
　　gave me inspiration
Oh, this life just isn't right

I'm not even supported in a proper chair
In this one I slip and slide
But my nurse's aide is great at doing my hair
And recreation therapy gives me pride

I feel supported by professionals; they know I need more
Their honesty I adore
So time to open a new door…and unlock the key to this
　　mystery

One week later and not any better
My hair is finally done and cut
It's snow and frigid weather
Still using my beauty to shake my booty butt
More hypotonia[56] and all the dysphonia is not phony
Hearing the words "I can't help you yet"
This all sounds like yucky baloney
I will always forgive but never forget

The feeling of burning on the inside
And freezing on the outside

I guess it's up to me to give more of me
But what am I giving lately?

Besides frustration, confusion, and ache
I want to give more than I can take

***

As Jessica puts it for me:

Through this journey, my feelings are still changing. New feelings are always being created, allowing me to discover mental and emotional depths I never realized I had. In the hardest and most painful of times, I was experiencing a level of emotion that brought out the most profound thoughts. I was forced to ask the hard questions (to myself and others). All the confusion and even doubts opened the door to expansive thinking and so much more writing. I began this book in May of 2016 without even knowing where I was going to be. I was given more to work with; more substance to mold (and feel). I feel my mind is triumphing amid the afflictions, stepping up where other abilities may lack. And I will never stop questioning. Therefore, I will never stop learning; changing; growing; sharing.

***

Right now, I still have wonder...

How? Who? What? Where? When? "Why? There are so many questions throughout life that we have, and most of them do not get answered. However, finding an answer to a problem is one of the greatest feelings. Is the answer always a solution? I do not think so. I'm not sure about most things. Though I do try to make explanations from what is given.

My little cousin, Marie, was one of those kids who would respond with "Why?" every time someone answered her initial question. The whys can be endless. This makes me realize there is still so much to question. There is always something that remains unknown, always something left to discover. As scary as it may feel, I realized the unknown is a gift to experience the D.A.N.C.E. in a new way.

How do you really feel? Is it overwhelming? Do you bottle things within or let them go? Please know whatever you are feeling is valid, and it's how you D.A.N.C.E. with them to get through every day.

Chapter 22
The Gift

Unwrapping a present without ripping the package can be the most difficult part of the gift giving process.

"Is this for me?"
"Really? It's free?"
"Thank you so much."
"Here, this is for you."

EVERYTHING IN LIFE BEGINS AND ends before it begins again. We must wrap a gift and close it with pride. Things are wonderful reminders that actual presence is a gift—one that cannot have a price tag on it. I am always amazed at the fact that every single person in the universe lives and leaves with a different package of feelings, experiences, and circumstances. It creates an opportunity for new human gifts to be born. Giving (and being) a gift that goes outside of the box and having extra baggage makes it more exciting to unwrap more.

To celebrate this, commodities of enjoyment, sentiment, and function are given in appreciation. The thought behind it is what makes it special. My family lives for giving gifts! My mom is truly like Mrs. Claus all year long. Giving is an even greater gift than receiving, and it's usually reciprocal. My hospital/rehab rooms were always filled to the max with presents that recognized my presence, making me feel loved. Still even a million comfy items, fuzzy socks, blankets, and sweaters (my favorite present) cannot replace the comfort of having a loved one around or even a kind stranger who may turn into one of my loves. You never know when someone might turn out to be the gift of a lifetime.

Do you think the gifts we receive are coincidental? I believe each skill, passion, and even material thing can have a strong purpose in your life. For example, fellow brain injury survivor Lisa Farinelli expressed the concept Coincidence or God Incidence? in 2018 at a PeaceLove event run by another CREATOR, Valerie. This saying and the story behind it has had great significance in my life. For instance, a brain-injury walk led Lisa to us, thus allowing her to become a participant of expressive arts activities, which I ran (through PeaceLove) for my organization. This allowed her to finally open up and embrace her gifts of creativity. With help from other therapies as well, she continued to ask herself if the events that occur in life happen for a reason.

I think there are connections everywhere. If there's ever a relation between two things, I like to think of the relation as that of a ship on the sea; waters can be tested to let a relationship ride. Realistically, every person or thing we come across is not always going to have a huge impact on our lives; coincidental occurrences are a part of life. However, I think a God incident happens if a presence is made known in a bigger way; it's a gift that can be used as an act of faith and love for good. Even tragedy, beneath horror and grief, gives a person a gift to make a positive change personally and socially. If my experiences did not happen, you would not have this book to read or quote from.

Each day there are gifts like these to embrace, even if they are not what I once hoped for. Fittingly, I have always loved calendars and planners to help me keep track of life in a fun way. A calendar has every day of the week with dates for an entire year. But when a calendar year ends, does it really end? Not in our memories. Some people are able to remember more than others—not just for special dates, but for every single day. Similar to my brother Lawrence, my good friend Colin remembers all the dates of everything done and knows the days of the week people were born on. This is an ability to be treasured for life. Lawrence and Colin both boggle my mind with their genius abilities. I think that's why when plans change, they have a harder time adapting because they truly do embrace the moments—the fleeting gifts.

Though memories fade as well, some things are unforgettable. I met Colin at a Dare to Dream conference for high school students who have disabilities, where we both represented our school by giving a motivational presentation. Now Colin is one of my best guy friends. Colin was adopted from an orphanage in Romania when he was seven. He is extremely funny, personable, hardworking, social, and intelligent, despite having some developmental delays and learning disabilities. He definitely lights up our parties, gatherings, and talent shows with his presence. He still has so much to give. The calendar never ends with Lawrence and Colin, as their gifts are to cherish each day of life's gift.

Considering all this, why does it seem like some people are extra gifted with special talents? I believe that some just find it and embrace it sooner or more openly. I think passion is what elevates a power to the next level. I learned as I grew older that it's okay if you're not talented at something. To participate in an activity is priceless in itself. Comparison of your life to others' is a toxin many of us carry with us. Side effects include not fully living and not fully loving your own life.

Moment in Time

How is life a gift when so many face challenges? When these challenges make living each moment with joy and gratitude a struggle? My answer is momentum—helped by motivation. It gets us going even if the speed is slow. By definition, momentum is literally "strength or force gained by motion or by a series of events."[57]

In the hospital, several months into having my movement disorder, I wanted to understand the PUNch line of the scribbly zigzag my life was becoming. I wanted to climb that mountain, seemingly further than ever. I thought to myself, *How can I mount inevitability on a mountain?*

So many times, I just feel like a floppy mess, but I have a MESSage to D.A.N.C.E. When life gives me less, movement is a LESSon to turn each moment into MOMENTum to COMe FORTh in the discomfort of all this. Each moment is a memory in the making. These memories follow us forever, stored somewhere in the universe, even without a picture or video. It's a movie that keeps moving. Once you think the climax is over, nope—the climb is not maxed out. There's only fast-forwarding or rewinding within the gift of the mind. Today—right now—this moment is your living gift.

All Good (March 19, 2019)

I cry
Every day
Not of sadness
Or joy
Yes, frustration
Makes a way
To communicate need
And emotion
Therapy: PT, OT, speech
Nurses; suction
Waiting for results
Then decide?
What to do
Tricky
I have
No balance
I do yoga
Movement out of control
I dance
No more speech
I make bigger statements
Tight tremors in thumb
Write loosely
Patience
Jerk, spaz, wail
Well…soul sings

Hallelujah
Doing best I could
Cuz my loves
Giving to others
Motivations
It's all good

My condition continues to decline, making this more difficult to complete. I'm blessed to have an amazing support system. Shortly before the tremors in my hand increased, I wrote the following song. My talented music therapist, Samantha, composed the melody. We performed it at our seventh annual talent show on March 11, 2019.

Mirror Calls

How can we explain the unexplained?
Healing when heel keeps going down?
When will it come? Can it be sustained?
Waiting and waiting and waiting
But what if it's all around?

I hear, see, and I feel
My God's healing is real
Third time's the charm
Or three strikes you're out?

Thanks for your alarm
Creating what it's all about…

So hey…
Mirror…calling me
Reflection I can't see
Magic dancing in mystery
Miracle, ooh…miracle, ooh…miracle, ooh
Image comes silently

Mirror calls...
Imagine

Sometimes it's in the small everyday
The ability to love that makes it OK
So I'm waiting but it's not weighted
Thinner than air...do you know it's there?

(Rap bridge):
Listen, God is by your side
Through the bumpy ride
All those tears you cried
Continue to fight with pride
Waiting for it...come in?
After a big loss, where's the big win?
Help me lift my chin
Up...Do you see my grin?

Mirror, mirror calling me
Reflection I can't see
Magic dancing in mystery
Miracle, ooh...miracle, ooh...miracle, ooh
Image comes silently
The mirror calls
Imagine

It's moving to soothe the why
Why? Your answer doesn't lie
Awake truth hidden away
Coming up to tell the world

Hey...
Mirror, you're calling me
From a reflection I can't see
There's magic in the mystery
Miracle, ooh...miracle, ooh...miracle, ooh

Image comes silently
Imagine when the mirror calls…
Ooh…

***

After some reflection of your own, you're probably wondering why there are twenty-two chapters in this book. (The numbers 2, 2, and I always felt more confident in a tutu). Just kidding…let's keep it real.

Real 22

> *A cheerful heart is good medicine.*
> —*Proverbs: 17:22*

Twenty-two is my special number because it has been showing up inexplicably for me my entire life, and especially since I turned twenty-two. This number represents the cheerful heart given to me by the Holy Spirit that keeps me alive; it is the best medicine I could ever receive. "When we see this number regularly, it means we have a strong calling to achieve our soul's purpose, and the plans that are in progress are for something that will benefit humanity or Mother Earth."[58]

I was born on June 22, 1995, and in 2017, I turned twenty-two. It is considered a miracle number in the Bible, as the significance of the number shows up repeatedly. It symbolizes light and revelation. The Hebrew alphabet is made up of twenty-two letters, which can also represent elements of creation. "Additionally," the number is a double 11 (said to symbolize disorder and chaos), implying a concentration of disorganization. That sums me up fittingly.

For my twenty-second birthday weekend, Jessica, my college best friend Archeline, and I went to New York City for an escape room experience and then to Chinatown for dinner. We were so close to finishing our space shuttle escape but ended up running out of time. We were missing one number: two. The code to save the planet was 2424. Then I received my fortune cookie, which, as always, had twenty-two in the lucky numbers section, along with twenty-four. Little signs everywhere, always. That was an incredible night, yet I felt like it was a race against time—kind of like life.

There is also a thing called catch-22, which is considered "a problematic situation for which the only solution is denied by a circumstance inherent in the problem or by a rule."[59] Basically, it's an unsolvable, paradoxical circumstance. So maybe I am in a catch-22. I need to move to live, but movement exacerbates my symptoms. I take these setbacks as signals and signs.

Twenty-two is a gift; it brings such hope, reminding me each day is a miracle. It might seem like we are running out of time, not a second to waste. A cheerful heart will make each second we caught the twenty-two worth the miracle mile.

It All Adds Up

I'll leave off with another significant connection to counting my days. As I mentioned above, the number 11 comes into play for me inevitably—a symbol of yet more hope.

> *Now faith is the substance of things hoped for, the evidence of things not seen. (Hebrews 11:1 KJV)*

Here is an edited version of a blog entry from the eleventh anniversary of my accident:

11 Years (June 1, 2019)

11 seconds hit
11 minutes hurt
11 hours holding on
11 days hopeful
11 weeks home
11 months humbled

Turned to years of high healing and happiness
Now 11 years HERE, but…
HOW?

Does the miracle of movement bring me back to life, then get flipped upside down, turning my mind and body away from each other?

Amara-versary is a term used to celebrate my survival and thriver-ship after being struck by a car. This year hits harder than the myoclonic jerks.[60] So many questions and, well, answers—God gives to me through love. That's all I need in this real reality show of Amara's Dance with the greatest cast possible, who never left, who came after my fall and stayed with no obligation.

11 is half of 22. God giving…
And 24, I will soon be living
It's in the numbers' infinity
Words of eternity
Music's harmony
Art's imagery
Dance's abilities
Life's mysteries

This makes my spirit strong most of the time and makes me say "Love you" repeatedly in my slurred, ataxic, distorted way that few understand. Rare neurological injuries and illnesses have controlled much of me, especially recently. I wake with a happy heart because of all I was. That helps me now, making my future less scary. D.A.N.C.E. forever.

Right now, in bed I need help and hope, but having strength to write this should clarify I am okay even when I'm not.

Discover, Accomplish, Nourish, Create, Embrace. If you want to help me find eleven reasons to D.A.N.C.E., share your gift.

God bless us, as we are all hit by something all the time.

***

It's a year later now, and I am wrapping up this chapter. After countless doctor visits, hospital testing, and rehabilitation, did I get my miracle of a diagnosis or treatment? Well, no. But it's okay, as I am finally fully accepting this reality.

Throughout the four years of writing this book—and all my life's journey—I learned that the greatest gifts are the invisible bows that tie us all together: the ribbons of connection. Maybe these subtle but powerful connections are in the rain, the wind, the fire, and even our passion or the massive yet mysterious magic that moves it all. Acceptance, adaptability, and art (triple *A*, ay!) help drive the disorderly motions out of my mind box to dancing with my present package and everyone I love endlessly.

I'm grateful people always want to help me. I always say the greatest gift is being a friend—not only of others to me, but to themselves and others. My struggles have offered me the opportunity to present my experiences to the world and share perspectives I wouldn't have had otherwise. My heart has only grown.

I think my brain (ironically my biggest problem) is my God-given gift, because although parts of it are not in tune with my body, I can still feel for others emotionally (maybe even on a deeper level), think abstractly, embrace humor, and cognitively reconstruct my thoughts, as if the creative parts of me have kicked into high gear. This gift is always changing. I work hard to keep it intact so I can continue to be a supportive friend and loving person—displaying my motto of D.A.N.C.E. for all.

I am forever changed. Although I have faced losses, I have gained so much more.

I think this book is a miracle—AMARAcle. It reflects who I am on the inside, which not one person can see due to my outer appearance these days.

This is why…

A gift with no return or exchange
The D.A.N.C.E. is priceless
More time to arrange
Your story to express

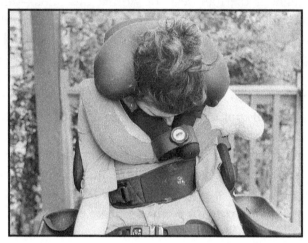

Amara, 2020

***

You have a special gift, Amara. (Uncle Neil Giannone)

D.A.N.C.E. and Beyond

THE END OF 2019 TO the beginning of 2020 was filled with traumatic experiences at numerous facilities. After all the doctors' appointments (many times elusive and constantly rescheduled), severely bumpy travels, exhausting therapy sessions, and overstimulation from inevitable complications (and even good things), what I realized was that I just needed to be home.

What I can say right now is that I am not giving up on life by not going to doctors, therapies, and community gatherings (well, as I'm writing this, everyone has joined me in quarantine). Nor am I giving up on life by refraining from searching for answers. I am giving myself life by living happily in an adaptive environment, shaded in my bed where my body is supported and functions.

> *Anyone, no matter what his or her circumstance is, can spend years looking for the right answers. How can you get by? What will become of you? How can you make a difference? All the while, time passes, and the magic that shapes the tiny folds of our days is tucked between passing smiles, words of encouragement, moments with loved ones; silent journeys in solitude; imagination; connection. Our impact is subtle, but grand. (Jessica Giannone)*

Spiritually, through all this, I found all the answers I needed: the significance of precious time and spending it the best I can. I sing, dance, and tumble in my mind often. In my dreams, I focus on ballet and acrobatic techniques I never mastered. COVID-19 heightened my gratitude; with my strong lungs, I breathe prayers for healing and happiness of the world.

Maybe this lesson is: life is going to move and shift, but it does not take away love. Love is the constant.

It's mind-boggling how details really don't matter to depict the essence of a whole story. At the same time, paying attention to the essential details tells the story. My story and its message is meant to be broad—filled with many different meanings. My goal is always to connect—just like music and dancing—moving boundlessly with all the people I love. Together, this connected love, it will abound.

This is why I *D.A.N.C.E.* I know you can **dance** too.

Resources

Riccio Pick-Me-Ups sites:
ricciopickmeup.org
facebook.com/RPMU1

Amara Riccio sites:
Amarariccio.weebly.com
Instagram: @dancewithamara
CaringBridge: @dancewithamara

Jessica Giannone sites:
jmgiannone.com
medium.com/@giannonej1

Mentioned in Book

Cristabelle Braden (inspirational music/podcast)
cristabellebraden.com

Fighting H.A.R.D. Foundation (rare disease and chronic illness)
fightinghardfoundation.org

Dream Factory (children's wish organization)
dreamfactoryinc.org

PeaceLove (mental wellness nonprofit)
peacelove.org

Mosaic Music Therapy (Samantha Dean, my therapist)
mosaicmusictherapy.com

CFC Loud N Clear Foundation (addiction recovery)
healingus.org

Operation Beachhead (adaptive sports)
opbeachhead.org

Be the Change NJ (community service nonprofit run by my professor, Dr. Norma Bowe)
bethechangenj.org

Informative

Brain injuries
Biausa.org

Ataxia
Ataxia.org

Sexual assault
rainn.org/articles/sexual-abuse-people-disabilities

Mental health
nami.org

Lesley University Expressive Therapies
lesley.edu/academics/explore/area-of-study/expressive-therapies/degree-level/graduate

ATRA (Recreational Therapy)
atra-online.com/page/AboutRecTherapy

More Helpful Resources

Chronic illness support
chronicloveclub.com

Disability resources/inspiration
yoocanfind.com/About

Empowerment fashion
girlschronicallyrock.com

Children's books/merchandise representing disabilities
theablefables.com

Resources and support for those with differences
differentandable.org

Terminologies of oppression
theantioppressionnetwork.com/resources/terminologies-of-
oppression/

Expressive arts exercises
expressiveartworkshops.com/expressive-art-resources/100-art-thera-
py-exercises/

Applications

Calm (meditation, mindfulness, sleep)

Spotify (music/podcasts) *See "This is Why I DANCE" playlist related to this book

The Mighty (support/health resource for people living with disabilities and illnesses)

Audible (audiobooks from *Amazon*)

Notes

[1] **Editor's Note**
Rise quote: Robert G. Ingersoll

[2] **Introduction (I...)**
Traumatic brain injury (TBI): A brain injury is any part of the brain damaged, whether because of an injury or illness. A traumatic brain injury is a blow or jolt to the head or a penetrating injury to the head that affects normal brain function. Severity can be mild (amnesia or unconsciousness) to severe, causing long-term functioning problems. A brain injury can also be acquired as a result of another medical condition. https://www.biausa.org/brain-injury/about-brain-injury/basics/overview ; http://www.biama.org/braininjury (accessed May 16, 2020).

[3] Diffuse axonal shearing: A shearing injury happens when tissue slides over tissue, which causes lesions that can lead to unconsciousness or a vegetative state. This type of injury also causes brain cells to die, leading to brain swelling. https://www.brainandspinalcord.org/diffuse-axonal-injury/ (accessed May 16, 2020).

[4] Diffuse encephalopathic slowing: Encephalopathy is a global cerebral dysfunction—activity slowing in the cortex. This can be a result of dysfunction of cortical neurons or abnormalities in subcortical gray or white matter. https://www.medlink.com/article/eeg_in_encephalopathic_conditions (accessed May 16, 2020).

[5] Ataxia: Ataxia is a lack of control over bodily movements. It is a rare, neurodegenerative disease. It affects muscles, which in turn alters a person's abilities such as walking, talking, swallowing, and fine motor skills. It is complicated to diagnose. https://ataxia.org/what-is-ataxia/ (accessed May 16, 2020).

[6] Pseudobulbar syndrome: Pseudobulbar palsy, or involuntary emotional expression disorder, affects a person's ability to control face muscles as well as the jaw, mouth, tongue, and throat. It can also impact a person's ability to speak, eat, and swallow. Other symptoms may be uncontrollable laughing or crying at inappropriate times. https://www.healthline.com/health/pseudobulbar-palsy (accessed May 16, 2020).

[7] Upper motor cranial nerve: The upper motor neuron (UMN) is within the central nervous system and controls voluntary movement and regulation of pos-

ture. https://www.sciencedirect.com/topics/neuroscience/upper-motor-neuron (accessed May 16, 2020).

[8] Kangaroo feeding pump: The Kangaroo ePump Enteral Feeding Pump provides continuous or intermittent feeding. https://www.cardinalhealth.com/content/dam/corp/web/documents/patient-recovery/Literature/kangaroo-epump-enteral-feeding-pump-operation-and-service-manual.pdf (accessed May 16, 2020).

[9] Toxic iron buildup: Iron deposition in an injured brain can be from hemorrhages/microhemorrhages and is linked to various neurodegenerative conditions. https://www.ncbi.nlm.nih.gov/pmc/articles/PMC6306469/ (accessed May 16, 2020).

[10] **Part 1: Discover**
Discover definition: www.merriam-webster.com (accessed April 24, 2020).

[11] **Chapter 1: People, Places, and Things**
Autism: Autism spectrum disorder (ASD) is defined as a "complex developmental disability." Signs usually appear during early childhood and affect the person's ability to communicate and interact with people. https://www.autism-society.org (accessed May 16, 2020).

[12] Bipolar: Bipolar disorder is a mental illness that involves dramatic shifts in mood, energy, and (clear) thinking. People who have bipolar disorder experience unusually high moods (mania) and low moods (depression), with varying types of severity. https://www.nami.org/Learn-More/Mental-Health-Conditions/ (accessed May 16, 2020).

[13] Diabetes: Type 1 diabetes affects the body's ability to produce insulin, a hormone that the body needs in order to get glucose into the body's cells. Anyone, no matter what age, can get Type 1. https://www.diabetes.org/diabetes (accessed May 16, 2020).

[14] *Nature* definition: www.merriam-webster.com (accessed April 24, 2020).

[15] **Chapter 2: Diversity**
University of New Hampshire's Institute on Disability fact: "People with Disabilities are the Largest Minority Group in the US," Invisible Disabilities Association, referencing article from the Institute on Disability for the University of New Hampshire, https://invisibledisabilities.org/coping-with-invisible-disabilities/disability-benefits/disabilities-largest-minority-group-us/ (accessed May 16, 2020).

[16] Biopsychosocial: "Biopsychosocial model views health and illness behaviors as products of biological characteristics (such as genes), behavioral factors (such as lifestyle, stress, and health beliefs), and social conditions (such as cultural influences, family relationships, and social support)." https://courses.lumenlearning.com/boundless-psychology/chapter/introduction-to-health-psychology/ (accessed May 16, 2020).

[17] **Chapter 3: Passion**

Alzheimer's: Alzheimer's is a neurodegenerative disease that causes memory, thinking, and behavior problems. It is the most common form of dementia, which is a term used to describe a group of symptoms that entail memory loss and issues with cognitive abilities which affect everyday life. https://www.alz.org/alzheimers-dementia/what-is-alzheimers (accessed May 16, 2020).

[18] **Chapter 4: Education and Health**

World Health Organization information: World Health Organization Constitution, https://www.who.int/about/who-we-are/constitution (accessed May 16, 2020).

[19] Autonomic nervous system (dysfunction): The autonomic nervous system controls basic functions, such as heart and breathing rates, temperature, digestion, and sensation. Autonomic dysfunction happens when the nerves are damaged. The disorder can cause dizziness and fainting, abnormal sweating, exercise intolerance, urinary problems, digestion problems, and vision problems, among others. https://www.healthline.com/health/autonomic-dysfunction (accessed May 16, 2020).

[20] Disabilities fact: "What is an invisible disability?," Invisible Disabilities Association, https://invisibledisabilities.org/what-is-an-invisible-disability/ (accessed May 16, 2020).

[21] Complex regional pain syndrome (CRPS): "Complex regional pain syndrome (CRPS) is a form of chronic pain that usually affects an arm or a leg. CRPS typically develops after an injury, a surgery, a stroke or a heart attack. The pain is out of proportion to the severity of the initial injury." https://www.mayoclinic.org/diseases-conditions/crps-complex-regional-pain-syndrome/symptoms-causes/syc-20371151 (accessed May 16, 2020).

[22] Errors in health care: Ray Sipherd, "The third-leading cause of death in US most doctors don't want you to know about," CNBC, published February 22, 2018, https://www.cnbc.com/2018/02/22/medical-errors-third-leading-cause-of-death-in-america.html (accessed May 16, 2020).

[23] Myoclonus: Myoclonus is defined as a sudden muscle spasm; involuntary and uncontrollable. It can involve one or a group of muscles. https://www.healthline.com/health/myoclonus (accessed May 16, 2020).

[24] Rare disease information: "Rare Disease Facts," National Organization for Rare Disorders, published February 1, 2019, https://rarediseases.org/wp-content/uploads/2019/02/nord-rareinsights-rd-facts-2019.pdf; Lisa Sencen, "Early Diagnosis: Perspectives from NORD Student Chapter Leader, Harjot Randhawa," National Organization for Rare Disorders, posted January 18, 2018, https://rarediseases.org/early-diagnosis-perspectives-from-nord-student-chapter-leader-harjot-randhawa/; "What Is a Rare Disease?," Rare Disease Day, https://www.rarediseaseday.org/article/what-is-a-rare-disease (accessed May 16, 2020).

[25] Gastroparesis: Gastroparesis alters the normal movement of stomach muscles. It can cause problems with digestion, nutrition, and blood sugar, as well as cause nausea, vomiting, and numerous other stomach issues. https://www.mayoclinic.org/diseases-conditions/gastroparesis/symptoms-causes/syc-20355787 (accessed May 16, 2020).

[26] Gastric pacemaker: A gastric pacemaker is used to treat gastroparesis. It's inserted into the abdomen and uses electrical wires that lead to the stomach, sending electrical impulses for stimulation after eating. https://www.nationwidechildrens.org/specialties/motility-center/motility-center-services/gastric-pacemaker (accessed May 16, 2020).

[27] **Chapter 5: Unseen Magic**
Brenè Brown quote: Brenè Brown, "Defining Spirituality," posted on her website March 27, 2018, first published in her book *The Gifts of Imperfection*, https://brenebrown.com/blog/2018/03/27/defining-spirituality/ (accessed May 16, 2020).

[28] Dysphonic: Dysphonia is when a person has difficulty producing normal sound. https://www.justintimemedicine.com/CurriculumContent/p/4916 (accessed May 16, 2020).

[29] **Chapter 6: Discover Yourself**
Atrophy: Muscle atrophy is "wasting or loss of muscle tissue." https://medlineplus.gov/ency/article/003188.htm (accessed May 16, 2020).

[30] **Part 2: Accomplish**
Accomplish definition: www.merriam-webster.com (accessed April 24, 2020).

[31] **Chapter 7: Confidence and Resilience**
Cristabelle Braden lyrics: Used with permission from Cristabelle Braden.

[32] AML leukemia: Acute myelogenous (or myeloid) leukemia (AML) is a cancer of blood and bone marrow. https://www.mayoclinic.org/diseases-conditions/acute-myelogenous-leukemia/symptoms-causes/syc-20369109 (accessed May 16, 2020).

[33] Cholangiocarcinoma: Cholangiocarcinoma is a rare cancer that forms in bile ducts. A bile duct is a tube that carries bile (fluid made by the liver) between the liver, gallbladder, and small intestine. https://www.cancer.org/cancer/bile-duct-cancer/about/what-is-bile-duct-cancer.html (accessed May 16, 2020).

[34] *Inspiration* definition: www.merriam-webster.com (accessed April 24, 2020).

[35] **Chapter 8: Everyday Achievements**
Neuro-ophthalmologist: Neuro-ophthalmology deals with visual symptoms (such as vision loss and issues with eye movement) that result from brain diseases. https://neurology.msu.edu/patient-care/neuro-ophthamology (accessed May 16, 2020).

[36] **Part 3: Nourish**
Nourish definition: www.merriam-webster.com (accessed April 24, 2020).

[37] Craniosacral therapy: Craniosacral therapy (CST) works with the body's soft tissue structures and the flow of cerebrospinal fluid between the head and spine

base to protect, support, and nourish the brain and spinal cord. https://my.clevelandclinic.org/health/treatments/17677-craniosacral-therapy (accessed May 16, 2020).

[38] Reiki: Reiki is a Japanese healing technique used for stress reduction, relaxation, and well-being. It treats the body, mind, emotions, and spirit. The person administering the treatment manipulates (with his or her hands) the life force energy flowing through the person's body. https://www.reiki.org/faqs/what-reiki (accessed May 16, 2020).

[39] **Chapter 11: Mind**
Maniac: Lyrics from "Maniac" by Michael Sembello.

[40] *Crazy* definition: www.merriam-webster.com (accessed April 24, 2020).

[41] **Chapter 13: Leisure and Recreation**
Leisure: Based on information from *Introduction to Recreation and Leisure,* 3rd edition by Tyler Tapps and Mary Wells; publisher: Human Kinetics, Inc. (February 5, 2018).

[42] Recreation: Based on information from *Introduction to Recreation and Leisure,* 3rd edition by Tyler Tapps and Mary Wells; publisher: Human Kinetics, Inc. (February 5, 2018).

[43] **Chapter 16: Art**
Contraindications: "Something (such as a symptom or condition) that makes a particular treatment or procedure inadvisable." https://www.merriam-webster.com/dictionary/contraindication (accessed May 16, 2020).

[44] **Chapter 17: Connection**
Connection definition: www.merriam-webster.com (accessed April 24, 2020).

[45] Foreign accent syndrome: Foreign accent syndrome is a "speech disorder that causes a sudden change to speech so that a native speaker is perceived to speak with a 'foreign' accent." It's usually caused by brain damage, a brain injury, or a stroke. https://www.utdallas.edu/research/FAS/ (accessed May 16, 2020).

[46] **Chapter 19: Personal Creations**
Psychotherapy: Psychotherapy is talk therapy, which helps to treat mental illnesses and emotional problems. https://www.psychiatry.org/patients-families/psychotherapy (accessed May 16, 2020).

[47] Hemiparesis: Hemiparesis is weakness or an inability to move on one side of the body, affecting balance, coordination, and the ability to complete daily tasks. https://www.stroke.org/en/about-stroke/effects-of-stroke/physical-effects-of-stroke/physical-impact/hemiparesis (accessed May 16, 2020).

[48] **Chapter 20: The Journey**
Journey definition: www.merriam-webster.com (accessed April 24, 2020).

[49] Gastroesophageal reflux: Gastroesophageal reflux disease (GERD) is a digestive disorder caused by acidic stomach fluids backing up from the stomach into the esophagus. https://www.aaaai.org/conditions-and-treatments/related-conditions/gastroesophageal-reflux-disease (accessed May 16, 2020).

[50] Autoimmune thyroid condition: Hashimoto's thyroiditis is an autoimmune disorder that causes chronic inflammation of the thyroid. The condition affects the body's energy, temperature, and normal function of the brain, heart, muscles, and other organs. https://www.thyroid.org/hashimotos-thyroiditis/ (accessed May 16, 2020).

[51] Keppra: Keppra is an anticonvulsant drug used to control seizures; it has been shown to help reduce myoclonus symptoms. https://www.drugs.com/mcd/myoclonus (accessed May 16, 2020).

[52] Dysphagia: Dysphagia is when a person has difficulty swallowing. https://www.justintimemedicine.com/CurriculumContent/p/4916 (accessed May 16, 2020).

[53] **Chapter 21: The Feels**
"Phonia:" Dysphonia.

[54] "Phagia:" Dysphagia.

[55] "Arthria:" Dysarthria. It's when a person has difficulty with motor functions of speech production, forming and shaping sounds with the lips, tongue, and mouth. https://www.justintimemedicine.com/CurriculumContent/p/4916 (accessed May 16, 2020).

[56] Hypotonia: Hypotonia is when muscle tone is abnormally low, which causes diminished muscle resistance to passive stretching. https://www.biologyonline.com/dictionary/hypotonia (accessed May 16, 2020).

[57] **Chapter 22: The Gift**
Momentum definition: www.merriam-webster.com (accessed April 24, 2020).

[58] The number 22 information: Alex Myles, "The Reason we Keep Seeing the Numbers 2, 22, 222 or 2222," *Elephant Journal*, published February 22, 2017, https://www.elephantjournal.com/2017/02/reason-we-keep-seeing-the-numbers-2-22-222-or-2222/ (accessed May 16, 2020).

[59] *Catch-22* definition: www.merriam-webster.com (accessed April 24, 2020).

[60] Myoclonic jerks: See myoclonus.

About the Authors

AMARA ELISE RICCIO IS THE CREATOR and vice president of the nonprofit organization Riccio Pick-Me-Ups. It has been her life's dedication to provide aid and inspiration to individuals and families in need. She resides with her super parents, two quirky brothers, and two cats who keep them all sane—fulfilled at home in a whimsical room full of art, unicorns, teddy bears, medical equipment, the color pink, and all that jazz. Learn more at amarariccio.weebly. com.

Jessica Giannone is a full-time editor/ writer, word-puzzle maker, and singer. As a journalist and entertainer, she has produced and written visual, video, and audio content for magazines, newspapers, sketch shows, podcasts, and a hearty variety of online outlets. (When the band thing didn't work out, she returned to tinkering and overthinking.) She's a curious, energetic soul with a thirst for random knowledge and semi-eccentric adventures. In her spare time, she can be seen trying to get people to play Heads Up! and promoting the domestic value of fennec foxes…often daydreaming of intergalactic travel, speaking in pun, climbing trees, dragging her friends on elaborate hikes and food ventures, and quoting *Star*

Wars/The Wizard of Oz/Westworld/The Twilight Zone unapologetically. Learn more at JMGiannone.com.

  * Riccio Pick-Me-Ups is a 501(3)(c) nonprofit organization that provides educational, emotional, recreational, and financial support to families facing chronic medical hardships. Their mission is to provide inspiration and joy for people of all ages and abilities through arts and wellness programs.